PREPPER'S
HOME DEFENSE

PREPPER'S
HOME DEFENSE

Security Strategies
to Protect Your Family
by Any Means Necessary

Jim Cobb

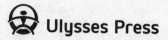 Ulysses Press

Published in the U.S. by
ULYSSES PRESS
P.O. Box 3440
Berkeley, CA 94703
www.ulyssespress.com

ISBN: 978-1-61243-115-4
Library of Congress Control Number 2012940427

Printed in Canada by Marquis Book Printing

10 9 8 7 6 5

Acquisitions Editor: Keith Riegert
Managing Editor: Claire Chun
Editor: Bill Cassel
Proofreader: Elyce Berrigan-Dunlop
Cover design: what!design @ whatweb.com
Photo credits: see page 222

Distributed by Publishers Group West

To Tammy,
Until the day after forever, sweetheart.

Contents

Acknowledgments

Writers often lament that it is a lonely business. The truth is, few writers would be successful without a rather large group of people working together behind the scenes.

To my beloved Tammy, thank you for all you have given up during the writing of this book. I truly and deeply understand and appreciate the efforts you've made to give me the time needed to work. To my boys, Andrew, Mike, and Tom, thank you for the times you were all able to be quiet and let me do what I needed to get this done. I love you all!

To Mom and Grandma, I wish you both were here to hold this book in your hands. I know you'd be proud of me. I miss you both terribly.

To Dad, thank you for your support and for always asking how the book was coming. I do so love our Sunday visits. Check it out, man!

To my in-laws, Jerry and Kathy, thank you for allowing me to be a part of your family. I hope I never let you down.

To Deborah in the UP, my partner in crime with www.SurvivalWeekly.com, your support and encouragement have been invaluable.

To my erstwhile cheerleaders, John Burks and Bob Freeman, your excitement about the book kept me going to the end.

To Rick Rourke, Rick Cox, and Jed Dronet, my erstwhile pre-readers, your input on the manuscript was much appreciated.

To Bob and Joanne Hrodey, a guy could hardly wish for better people to work for. Thank you both for putting up with me.

To Jerry Ahern, thank you for the Foreword. I wish you were here to see the final product. You were and still are an inspiration to many of us preppers and survivalists. May you rest in the peace you've truly earned.

To Scott Williams, thank you for your insight and advice while I was working on this book. Your input was truly beneficial.

To Ed Corcoran, thank you for giving me my start with writing about preparedness as a profession, rather than just a hobby. You gave me my start and for that I'll always be grateful.

To Steve Thibeault, just one more step in our plan for world domination! Thanks for your contribution to this work, as well as to my career. We're just getting warmed up!

To those who also contributed material to the book— Jon Merz, Chance Sanders, Laurie Neverman, Donald Jones—thank you for your assistance.

Special thanks to my editor, Keith Reigert. An author could hardly have asked for a more patient and helpful editor for his first book. Also, thank you to Kelly Reed

Acknowledgments

for sticking with me through the months of swapping book ideas. To all the folks at Ulysses Press, thanks for making this book so much better than it would have been without you.

To Chris Golden, thank you for holding my hand and teaching me about the business of writing. I hope you'll never regret not shoving me out from under your wing.

To Brian Keene, thank you for the best piece of writing advice I've ever received.

Last, but not least, a special thanks to one of my best mates, Ian Carter. Gone but certainly never forgotten.

Foreword

When Jim Cobb asked me to write an introduction for his book, I was extremely happy. I like Jim and his sensible approach to "prepping," which I still tend to call survival planning or something similar. Jim and I generally think quite a bit alike. Neither he nor I would ever advocate stockpiling weapons and ammunition while ignoring basic gardening, seeing to the water supply, elementary security concerns, etc.

Armchair preppers or survivalists have a great deal to learn once they wake up from their happy naps. Let's take guns. Everybody (almost) wants to talk about the guns. I like to talk about guns, too. Now, let's say you have decided that you like the AK-47—my choice in semi-auto only, of course—over the AR platform. One of your three children is old enough and reliable enough to carry a centerfire rifle. So, that's three AKs. I chose the Century International Arms Centurion 39. Using the postage scale, the rifle itself, devoid of accessories, weighs 7¾ pounds, while the magazine, thirty rounds loaded, weighs 2 pounds.

Let's say that your oldest child (the trustworthy one), your spouse and you yourself go it on the cheap and each only carry a rifle—loaded—and two thirty-rounders, not including the one in the rifle. So, that makes 7¾ pounds for the rifle and 2 pounds each for a loaded magazine. That adds up to 13¾ for the individual weapons package. A good camp and defensive knife will typically weigh 1¾ pounds, including sheath. Now we're at 15½.

Two pounds is the weight for a quart of water to carry on the belt. Let us assume that the canteen and its cover and possible canteen cup weigh so little that we can chart them off.

Now, remember, let's count a few pounds for clothes, boots, a couple of candy bars, and other miscellaneous items. Maybe we're at 20 pounds and we can proudly say that we have a grossly ill-equipped (not to mention probably ill-trained) member of the family who will be out of ammo and rendered totally ineffective as a combatant after the first encounter with an enemy of superior numbers and firepower.

Does your trooper have food and water waiting at whatever command and control center the good guys have established? Is there more ammo, either available in loaded magazines or loose?

Where do you locate resupply for food (beyond Hershey bars), medical supplies, water, toilet paper, flashlight batteries, etc?

What is your source for news and current information concerning the conflict? Is it to be trusted?

Foreword

This is only one out of a wide variety of scenarios the prepper might face. Smiling proudly at your tomato plants or your vast number of loaded rifle magazines isn't going to get you to the other side of whatever crisis it is that your group might have fallen into. Sure, preppers love those tomatoes, and plenty of spare magazines and lots of extra ammo can be comforting. But, there is a lot of other stuff for which the prepper needs to prepare—if he or she intends to really make it through the crisis, that is.

> —Jerry Ahern
> creator of The Survivalist book series,
> former president of Detonics USA,
> and author of hundreds of articles
> related to firearms and related gear

Introduction

If you do some searching at your local library or bookstore, you will no doubt discover that there have been dozens of books written on the general topic of home security. These books are full of suggestions on better locks, securing patio doors, and the pros and cons of alarm systems. Most have some great information and a few of those tips will even be shared in this book. However, all of these books are predicated on one fact: that Officer Friendly from your local police department will be able to help you in the event things go awry.

There are several potential scenarios that could cause a long-term lapse in social services like police and fire departments. Terrorists could finally get their hands on nuclear weapons, selectively detonating them in key locations across the country. A massive solar storm or an EMP burst could take down our electrical grid. The collapse of the U.S. dollar could bring our country to a standstill. A major earthquake along the New Madrid fault could decimate the Midwest. The Yellowstone caldera could finally give way, sending enough ash and debris into the atmosphere to cause a mini Ice Age.

Introduction

The rules will change substantially in the aftermath of an event of this magnitude. There will be no police officers coming to arrest the bad guys. There will be no S.W.A.T. teams to handle hostile situations. Dialing 911 just won't be an option. You will have to handle things on your own.

Most folks are genuinely good; they don't wish to harm anyone, let alone cause anyone serious injury or worse. But desperate times will make for desperate people. Think about it like this: What lengths might you go to in order to feed your family? There is an old saying that organized society is only nine meals away from anarchy. In other words, we're only three days removed from chaos. With that chaos will come changes in the personalities of the people around you. Behavior that was traditionally viewed as forbidden will now be rationalized in people's minds as being necessary for survival.

These changes in perception and behavior will necessitate a different approach to home defense and security. Where we may now feel reasonably secure by locking

our doors, after a societal collapse locked doors merely represent the initial stages of a defense plan. If there were a knock on your front door today, you'd probably peek out the peephole or window, then open the door to see who the person is and what they want. Post-collapse, you probably won't want to answer the door at all, or if you do, you will do so in a dramatically different fashion. In other words, your own behavior will need to change to reflect the realities of the new world. While you may not relish the idea of visiting harm upon another person, you may be forced to do so to preserve your own safety and well-being.

It is important to keep in mind that some of the suggestions contained in this book are patently illegal to implement in the eyes of the current court system. Of course, you probably don't have much need to build potentially lethal traps in your backyard right now. The key point here is that many of the techniques detailed here should not be used until and unless there comes a time when our current laws cease to exist. Engaging in illegal acts today will often lead to less-than-ideal outcomes, such as fines and/or imprisonment. Paying fines will certainly cut into your overall prepping budget and I doubt many people would like to take a chance on being locked in a jail cell during a societal collapse.

Of course, formulating a defense plan begs the question, from what or whom are you defending your home or retreat? Remember, we're concentrating on a post-collapse scenario. We're not concerned right now with the common burglar who is looking to snag your HD television. Instead, we are worried about people who truly wish to do you harm and take from you the basic necessities of life.

Essentially, there are four categories of aggressors you may face. As we progress through our discussion of post-collapse security and defense, you'll learn both general measures to be taken against all four threats as well as how each group should specifically be handled.

In the first category are the more or less normal people. These could be neighbors, friends, or perhaps strangers who are desperate for food and supplies and either know or suspect you have what they need. Typically, they will appeal to your compassionate side and you may feel compelled to help them out. That's your call to make and you'll have to take it on a case-by-case basis. But, generally speaking, think back to your days in grade school. If you don't have enough for the whole class....

The second category includes those who are commonly referred to in online forums as the MZBs (which stands for Mutant Zombie Bikers). This term arose out of the three most common villains in post-apocalyptic movies and books: the mutants in any number of low-budget science fiction movies, the zombies from shows like *The Walking Dead*, and the bikers from *The Road Warrior*. In reality, this term refers to those ne'er-do-wells who will travel in packs, pillaging the countryside. They will be fairly well organized and likely much more ruthless than the normal folks. Odds are good they will be well-armed and have experience using those weapons.

Third on our list are the power mongers. These are the people who hold at least a bit of local power now, such as

ACRONYMS

Preppers love acronyms. I'm not sure if this arises out of a desire to communicate through shorthand or because it makes emails and such sound more militaristic but whatever the cause, you're bound to come across dozens of acronyms and abbreviations on any survival-related website or message board. Here are a few of the most common ones in use today.

ATSHTF = After The Shit Hits The Fan

BOB = Bug-Out Bag

BOL = Bug-Out Location

BOV = Bug-Out Vehicle

CCW = Carry Concealed Weapon

EDC = Every Day Carry

FAK = First Aid Kit

GHB = Get-Home Bag

LEO = Law Enforcement Officer

MMW = Mad Max Wannabe

MZB = Mutant Zombie Biker

POTUS = President of the United States

SA = Situational Awareness

SCOTUS = Supreme Court of the United States

SERE = Survival Evasion Resistance Escape

SITREP = Situation Report

TEOTWAWKI = The End Of The World As We Know It

TSHTF = The Shit Hits The Fan

WCS = Worst Case Scenario

There are many other acronyms that are common online and not just in the realm of disaster readiness. These include:

AFAIK = As Far As I Know
BTDT = Been There, Done That
DD = Dear Daughter
DH = Dear Husband
DS = Dear Son
DW = Dear Wife
FIL = Father In Law
FS = For Sale
FWIW = For What Its Worth
HTH = Hope This Helps
IMHO = In My Humble/Honest Opinion
IRL = In Real Life
MIL = Mother In Law
OT = Off Topic
OTOH = On The Other Hand
PITA = Pain In The Ass
SO = Significant Other
TIA = Thanks In Advance
WTB = Want To Buy
YMMV = Your Mileage May Vary

law enforcement officers or government administrators. They are used to being in charge and will not want that to change. Because average citizens in their areas are used to seeing these power mongers as authority figures, it will often be fairly easy for them to consolidate the citizens under their "protection." The risk to the survivalist is that if a power monger learns of a stash of supplies nearby, he or she will go to great lengths to not only secure those supplies "for the common good," but also seek to instantly quell any potential rebellion, whether real or perceived.

Last, we have the psychotics. Now, before I get a ton of letters and emails dragging me over the coals, let me preface this by saying I fully realize the number of people suffering from potentially violent mental illness is quite small. But the fact is that they are present in our society today and most of them are treated with various prescription medications to keep their issues under control. Losing access to those meds will not only bring about withdrawal, it may cause a severe relapse. There will also be those for whom the disaster was too much to take and as a result suffer a significant break with reality, perhaps temporarily but possibly for the long haul. While probably much fewer in number than the MZBs, these folks who are suffering the effects of mental illness will pose a significant threat if only because it may be next to impossible to reason with them or convince them of genuine threats of bodily harm.

It is important to note that throughout the course of human history, no matter how bad a disaster or crisis may have been, eventually law and order were restored.

Introduction

Naturally, the larger the scope of the disaster, the longer it took for society to be reestablished. Hurricane Katrina was one of the largest natural disasters to ever strike the United States. It took several weeks before a semblance of "normal" life was restored to many of the affected areas. This is neither the place nor the time to debate how effective or ineffectual government agencies were during that process; the point is that order was eventually established. It didn't take decades, years, or even months. If an event on the order of a nationwide electrical grid failure were to happen, it might take years to recover, but rest assured, recovery would happen. In this book, we are concerned with the time frame that begins with the disaster and ends with order being restored.

Throughout this book, I will use the terms "prepper" and "survivalist" interchangeably. Typically, the difference between people who identify themselves as preppers versus survivalists tends to be their view on the role of firearms and security issues in their overall preparedness planning. Survivalists tend to devote considerable resources to amassing a substantial armory. Preppers, on the other hand, often view firearms as tools for acquiring food through hunting, rather than for defense. Of course, there is a lot of overlap between the two extremes and most folks would fall somewhere toward the middle of the spectrum. Because of this overlap, I don't see the terms "survivalist" and "prepper" as being mutually exclusive.

Often, we survivalists are dismissed as being "doom and gloomers" who pray for the end of the world. That is rarely the case. Most of us hope there will never come a time when we'll need to rely solely upon the food, water, and supplies we've set aside. We make plans as insurance against what might never happen. Home and retreat defense is merely one aspect of a comprehensive preparedness plan. Naturally, it is a vitally important component, since all the preps in the world will do you no good if someone takes them from you. With that said, it is my sincerest wish that you'll never truly need the information in this book.

SECTION I

SECURITY PLANNING

CHAPTER 1
Basic Security Concepts

There are several basic concepts common to all security plans, whether for a single-family home, a multi-acre retreat, or even an office building. One of the most fundamental aspects of security planning is the knowledge that no plan will ever be absolutely perfect. Given enough time and motivation, an aggressor will always be able to defeat any security plan. No lock is ever totally pickproof. No gate is ever really impregnable. Thus, the focus of an effective plan is to increase the amount of time and motivation necessary to defeat the plan.

Another key element to keep in mind is the motivation of your enemy. A sufficiently motivated attacker will voluntarily suffer even severe losses to his group, believing the efforts will be rewarded. Desperation is a powerful motivator. In a world without rule of law, as we saw in situations such as post-Katrina New Orleans, there will no doubt be large numbers of survivors seeking a meal, a bottle of clean water, and a safe place to rest. In even a short period of time, they will become desperate to acquire the basic needs of life. Your security plans should focus on dissuading these people from believing they can easily obtain these necessities from you.

In this chapter we'll look at a few of the fundamental principles you should keep in mind when designing your home security plan.

Deter, Delay, and Defend

The longer it takes for an attacker to get through your defensive measures, the more time you have to detect them and to implement additional security protocols. Conversely, the longer an attacker is able to operate undetected, the higher his chances of success. It is critical to be able to locate and take action against aggressors as soon as possible.

The amount of time it takes for an attacker to defeat both passive and active elements of your security plan is directly related to the number of those elements as well as their complexity. For example, climbing over a 5-foot

chain link fence takes only a few seconds for most people. But if that fence were instead 7 feet tall and topped with barbed wire, the amount of time it took to get over it would increase substantially. Anything you can do to increase the amount of time it will take an attacker to overcome or circumvent a defensive measure gives you more opportunity to take direct action against them.

Elevate Their Risk, Elevate Your Survival

Even if at a subconscious level, people make decisions on a risk versus reward basis. While the presence of a high fence topped with barbed wire would indicate to most people that there is something valuable inside, the presence of additional security measures may serve to cause potential aggressors to seek more vulnerable targets of opportunity.

When I was a young child, my father explained to me how best to deal with bullies. He said that if the bully felt he might be able to win the fight but would suffer moderate or severe injury in doing so, he would move on to someone else. The same principle applies here. If you give an aggressor reason to believe he will suffer a great loss just to gain entry, he will likely decide that the risk is too great for an unknown reward.

Control the Situation

Security, at the core, is all about control. If you were putting together a security plan for a large office building, for example, you would primarily be concerned with

LAYERED DEFENSE

One of the best ways to approach a security plan is to think in terms of layers. An attacker should have to somehow penetrate multiple layers or levels of security devices and protocols before reaching their final objective.

Take a piece of paper and draw an X in the center. Draw three circles around the X, each circle getting slightly larger. The outermost circle represents the area surrounding your home. This area is where you'll be patrolling and where you'll have in place fencing, barricades, and other fortifications, as well as your Early Warning Systems. The second circle is the walls, windows, and doors of your home. As we'll discuss, these will be fortified against entry. The innermost circle is your personal defensive measures, such as melee weapons and hand-to-hand combat skills. Between each of these distinct layers will be area denial devices and other surprises.

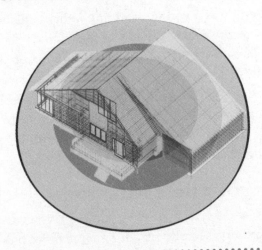

controlling access to the building itself, as well as to various departments within the organization. Today, this is usually accomplished through the use of electronic surveillance devices such as closed-circuit television. Often there will also be a badge key or even biometric devices used to unlock entrances to secured areas.

Similarly, for your retreat security plan you want to prevent unauthorized access to your home and ensure that items such as medical supplies and firearms are secured against both intruders and unauthorized members of your team. Of course, you probably won't be using biometric locks but instead relying upon more old-fashioned, yet tried-and-true measures such as hardened doors and windows.

In addition to access control, you also want to work toward maintaining control of an intruder's movements should they penetrate any level of your defenses. You want to successfully predict and control their actions every step of the way and counteract every option they may have. There is a fair amount of psychology involved with this. Fortunately, human beings are a fairly predictable lot. For example, given the choice between two paths, they will almost always choose the one that appears easier to travel.

Try this one the next time you are out for a drive with someone. When you get to a fork in the road, ask them to choose a direction. All other things being equal, most often people will choose the direction of their dominant hand. How is this useful in defense planning? Roughly

10 percent of the world's population is left-handed. So, as you lay out your plans for funneling your opponents to specific parts of your area of control, you know that the vast majority of people will choose to turn to their right if given a seemingly open choice.

Proactive, Reactive, and Flexible

A good security plan is both proactive and reactive. Your barricades are a *proactive* element. You've put them up ahead of any attacks in hopes of dissuading at least some potential aggressors. However, the way you handle someone who climbs over the barricade is *reactive*; you have a protocol in place that defines not only who responds to such an incident but also how the response should be carried out. No security plan is strictly proactive or reactive. Both elements need to be present for the plan to be successful.

It is also important that a degree of flexibility be built in to the overall security plan. An old military axiom states that no battle plan survives the first enemy encounter. What this means is that all the planning in the world could go right out the window if the enemy does not behave as expected. Therefore, a certain degree of improvisation will be necessary. You and your family need to understand that even if you've practiced a certain contingency a thousand times, when the time comes to do it for real, things aren't likely to go exactly as planned.

SITUATIONAL AWARENESS

Situational awareness—being vigilant about observing your surroundings—applies at both the individual and the group levels. When you are patrolling your area, you need to be aware of everything around you. Pay attention to sights, smells, and sounds. Take note of visible changes, such as vehicles that have been moved or previously unbroken windows that are now shattered. These sorts of changes may be indicative of new people being in the area and scouting for supplies. If they find your group, they will probably become very interested in what you may have to offer them.

Your group members need to be extremely observant about the area immediately surrounding your location. By maintaining lookouts and patrols as the situation permits, you'll be in a much better position to proactively curtail possible threats. With that said though, a key element of situational awareness is to strive for threat avoidance whenever possible. You and your team should not go out looking for battle. Remember, every physical conflict carries with it the risk of injury, no matter how outnumbered or outgunned your opponent may appear to be. I'm not saying you shouldn't stand your ground if attacked. The idea of threat avoidance is to steer clear of conflicts until and unless you have no other option.

GOOD COMMUNICATION

On a group basis, situational awareness involves excellent communication among group members. You should

RICK RESCORLA: DRILL LEADER, HERO

Consider the case of Rick Rescorla. He was the security chief for financial services firm Morgan Stanley in the Twin Towers during the terrorist attacks on 9/11. For several years prior to the attacks, Rescorla had conducted regular evacuation drills for all employees. While these drills were not looked upon favorably by upper management because they disrupted the workday, Rescorla insisted they be done.

When the attacks occurred, his drills had the desired effect: The close to three thousand employees in both towers immediately began to evacuate in an orderly fashion. Rick Rescorla's insistence on practicing the evacuation procedures to the point of rote memorization saved the lives of all but thirteen employees.

Every defense protocol should be drilled and practiced on a regular basis. Every action should be rehearsed again and again. If it just isn't feasible to expect a member of your family to make a run from the house to a guard post in less than a minute, the time to discover this is during a drill, not a real attack.

develop some sort of system by which you can keep each member of your group informed of patrol observations. This may be as simple as jotting notes in a collective notebook that is reviewed by all patrol members prior to embarking on their shift. In fact, you should consider drawing maps of the area, noting landmarks to help with orientation when in the field. You could set this up on a dry-erase board and make changes as necessary after each patrol.

Group awareness also extends to communication with neighbors and other trusted people in your area. By fostering a network of contacts throughout your area, you will greatly increase the amount of information available to you and your team. Work out a system with these contacts whereby you are able to regularly trade information with them. This may be done through regular meetings or by simply passing information from house to house.

Drill, Drill, and Drill Again

Drills are an extremely important component of any successful plan, yet it is the area most often lacking. Plans are really nothing more than theory waiting to be put into practice. Drills allow you to modify your plans, see what works and what doesn't, and adapt accordingly.

Furthermore, practicing your plans and conducting regular drills will ingrain the proper actions into you and your family. Quite often during a crisis, people tend to freeze up if they haven't been taught what to do in the situation. However, with the proper training and practice, their bodies will just naturally perform the required actions with little or no thought.

CHAPTER 2
Operations Security

Operations security, known in military jargon as OPSEC, is the first—and possibly most important—layer of defense. Simply put, OPSEC refers to keeping your mouth shut about what you have stockpiled and what other preparations you've made toward surviving a disaster. In other words, "loose lips sink ships." Every person who knows about your preps is one more person who could come looking to take what you have, whether through pleading or by force. Furthermore, each person who knows about your stockpiled supplies could conceivably tell several other people, thus dramatically increasing your overall risk level.

There are two sides to OPSEC: before and after the collapse. Pre-collapse OPSEC will focus on keeping your preparations as quiet as possible. After a collapse, you will most likely want to continue focusing on remaining quiet and out of sight, though there are divergent schools of thought on this, as we shall see.

Pre-Collapse OPSEC

As you go about making your preparations for post-collapse survival, you will naturally accumulate a fair amount of supplies. Unless you live far out into the sticks, you have neighbors and they have eyes and ears. They will undoubtedly notice a sudden increase in the number of packages arriving on your doorstep. They will also likely notice a dramatic increase in the number of trips you make to the grocery store or Sam's Club, especially if it is just you and your spouse living at home. You could try convincing your neighbors you've taken in a teenage foreign exchange student but odds are that won't fly.

SHOPPING

When it comes to local shopping, your best bet is to spread out your purchases. While you want to be sure you're getting the best prices and shopping the sale ads, don't go overboard if you can avoid it. For example, if canned tuna is on sale and this is something you may be low on, go ahead and stock up on several cans, but avoid buying a case or two at a time. Unless the store is very far from home, you can always make another trip or two. If, on the other hand, the store is someplace you only get to once a month, you're probably safe in stocking up with a large purchase.

If you have an attached garage, make a habit of pulling your car into it and closing the door before unloading your purchases. First, this is safer from a personal security standpoint as walking into an open garage and subduing a resident while they are getting out of their car is a favorite technique of some home invasion criminals. Second, this approach keeps neighbors and passers-by from seeing exactly what you bought.

Trust me, even the most disinterested neighbors will remember seeing you bringing home case on top of case of canned soup, especially if this is something you just started doing. While they might write you off as being the neighborhood kook for the time being, post-collapse they will almost surely come knocking on your door looking for a handout or perhaps more.

STORAGE

As your food and supply stores increase, you may have to get creative with storage. We'll talk about hidden and secure storage in a later chapter; suffice it to say here that you don't want your cases of toilet paper and buckets of rice sitting in the middle of your living room. Personally, I've always felt that prepping should not hinder a family from living their day-to-day lives. It is difficult to sit down and watch a movie as a family if you need to shift around a dozen cases of butt wipe just to see the TV. Few people want to live like they belong on an episode of a show on hoarding. Not only is it poor OPSEC, it is just unsafe.

Post-Collapse OPSEC

When it comes to OPSEC in a post-collapse world, there are two schools of thought. One says that you should live as invisible an existence as possible and try to make your home look abandoned. The other school of thought is to project a strong defense, almost as if daring someone to

An abandoned-looking home may be just as much of a deterrent to intruders as a heavily fortified one.

try something. As discussed in Chapter 1, a target that looks like it could present problems may convince potential aggressors to move on to the next one. However, this approach carries with it the risk that, sooner or later, someone will accept the dare. It could end up being more trouble than it is worth.

The strategy you choose will depend on your location and the circumstances of the actual collapse. If you are in an urban or suburban area, odds are pretty good that you'll have neighbors who will be struggling to survive. You can do anything you want to your home to make it look burned out and abandoned, but these people will know you are still occupying the structure. Unless you can get the entire neighborhood to go along with the ruse, the idea is something of a non-starter.

My suggestion is, after taking the specific situation and details into account, work on surviving while leaving as little of a footprint as possible. What do I mean by footprint? For example, don't let it be known that you have food when others are going hungry. Keep your empty tin cans under wraps. Burn paper packaging in your woodstove or campfire. If times are truly desperate, consider reducing your diet so you don't stand out as being particularly well fed when others are punching new holes into their belts so they can keep their pants from landing around their ankles.

Give some thought to what will likely be the day-to-day activities of a post-collapse existence and work on solving the "footprint" problem before the need to do so becomes critical. For example, burning large piles of trash would indicate that the inhabitants are well fed enough to not only create such piles of trash, but also to spend the time necessary to burn it, rather than spending every waking moment acquiring food. However, letting bags of trash pile up would not only have a similar effect, but also invite vermin. For these reasons, you'll need to stay on top of trash disposal. Paper items can be burned in the fireplace or woodstove. Metal and glass containers could possibly be repurposed for water storage. Plastic trash could be buried, provided you have the space to dig a pit.

LIGHT DISCIPLINE

Large rolls of landscape fabric can be used as blackout curtains at night. Having these hanging over the inside of your windows will allow you to use oil lamps and candles without the light being visible outside the home, which might attract travelers passing by at night.

If you need to venture outside at night and it is necessary to use a flashlight, fixing a red filter on the lens will reduce the visibility of the light at a distance. Another method to accomplish the same goal is to take a piece of cardboard and cut out a circle the same size as the flashlight lens. Make a very small hole in the center of the cardboard, maybe ⅛ inch or so, and tape the cardboard over the lens. The hole allows plenty of light for you to see what you need to see, yet there is very little light visible even at a small distance away.

NOISE DISCIPLINE

Frequent, extended use of a generator will undoubtedly attract quite a bit of attention from neighbors as well as those who just happen to be in the area. The sound of a generator signals two things: first, that you have a generator, and second, that you have fuel for it. Only use such devices when absolutely necessary. If using a generator is part of your overall disaster plan, consider rigging up some sort of sound-dampening shroud over it. While you'll never be able to get it to be truly silent, anything you can do to reduce the inevitable noise will be of benefit.

ODOR DISCIPLINE

The odor of steaks grilling on the back patio could be detected from quite a ways off. The same goes for burning trash and wood fires. However, this would actually be less of a consideration in an urban environment than out in the sticks. In a post-collapse city, the odor of sewage, burning buildings, and the piles of debris will likely mask the smells of cooking, at least beyond close distances.

With that said, though, take logical precautions. Don't spend any more time than absolutely necessary cooking a meal outside, where the mouth-watering scent of char-ring meat can travel. Be aware that the more spices you use in your cooking, the easier it may be to detect. Some spices, such as curry, can be smelled for days after they have been used.

Maintaining proper OPSEC both now and after a crisis hits will go a long way toward reducing your potential risks. If people are in the dark about your preps, they have little reason to poke around further. Remember, motivation is one of the key elements in an attack. Reduce the motivation and you'll reduce the risk.

SECTION II

PHYSICAL DEFENSE

CHAPTER 3
Perimeter Defense

The security measures at your perimeter are the first physical defenses an intruder will encounter. The hope is that they will stop there, though of course you should plan as if they won't. It is important to recognize that your perimeter isn't limited to just an imaginary line surrounding your home or retreat. Instead, as we discussed earlier, you should incorporate different layers within your perimeter. Think of it more like the track at your local high school. Your home lies at the center of the grass infield of the track, with the paved track marking the perimeter. To continue with that analogy, the perimeter should consist of several "lanes" of security measures, each of which is a layer in your security.

There are three essential types of defenses to incorporate into your perimeter. *Obstacles* are those things that will slow or stop an attacker, such as barriers. *Detection systems* include things like alarm systems and other early warning measures. The third element is the *response* by you and your team to the threats as they reveal themselves.

45

Defining the Perimeter

The first step in defending your perimeter is to define it. The area to consider your perimeter is everything extending outward from your doorstep. You'll need to take a good, hard look at your specific location and take into account the realistic capabilities of your team to determine where your perimeter ends. Obviously it can't go on to the horizon in most cases. But in a rural area, the perimeter might extend a couple hundred yards or more in every direction. In an urban area it will probably be no more than a couple hundred feet at best.

You need to be brutally honest with yourself when it comes to this aspect of security planning. It would be a costly mistake to believe that you, your spouse, and two kids can realistically secure a perimeter that extends for thousands of yards in every direction. There will end up being too many gaps in the perimeter, gaps that will be exploited at some point. Define your perimeter as an area where you can truly plug all holes and stop all but the most determined attackers.

Keep in mind as well that in a post-collapse world, you may not need to take property lines into account. If the homes on every side of you are abandoned, you might consider extending your perimeter to include them. Even if they are occupied, you should approach them and discuss incorporating their yards and property into your perimeter.

Obstacles

Obstacles are generally passive defenses. Some obstacles are there just to delay and frustrate aggressors. Others are intended to funnel the attackers to an area you can better control.

The ideal would be to surround your home with concrete walls that are a dozen feet high and a few feet thick, topped with razor wire, with a strong metal gate providing access in and out. However, I can just imagine how that suggestion would be met at the family dinner table on Sunday evening. Realistically though, there are several options available for constructing fencing and other barriers.

HEDGES

Provided you have the land to do so, you could start with a nice thick hedge. Boxwood is one great option for this purpose. When you think of the large topiary sculptures or even mazes, these are often boxwood. They can grow to about 15 feet tall. While a hedge of boxwood or any other plant won't stop a truck, remember the point of obstacles is to slow down your attacker so you have time to react. A truck coming at your perimeter will be easily detected either way, right? The idea here is to *funnel* your attackers to areas you can more easily control.

Another advantage of natural barriers like hedges is that they won't look out of place in most locations. It will not give the impression that you have anything to hide, now or later.

Bamboo is another excellent natural barrier. It grows rather tall quite quickly and when planted close together, it creates a fence that requires considerable effort to breach.

FENCES

One of the most inexpensive fences would be chain link. However, for security purposes, you get what you pay for. Even a moderately determined intruder could scale a chain link fence in a matter of minutes. Top it with barbed wire or razor wire and you'll add difficulty, but it will still not be insurmountable in the long run. A minute or two with a pair of bolt cutters would be all it would take to make a slit large enough to slip through. But that minute or two may be enough for you to take further action.

Another option is to build your fence out of wood. Still not too expensive but realistically it is even easier to defeat than chain link. An axe or chainsaw, while noisy, will make short work of a wooden fence. Plus, it is difficult and much more pricey to build a fence high enough to reasonably consider it secure.

WALLS

Brick and concrete walls are excellent options for security, but you'll pay through the nose unless you're able to do the work yourself. That would not be recommended unless you truly know what you're doing. Topping it with broken glass embedded in the concrete is a traditional touch and does work well. But a nice, thick concrete wall probably won't go over very well with the homeowner's association, condo board, or neighbors. Just food for thought.

SANDBAGS AND DEBRIS

Given time and effort, as well as a bit of preplanning, the urban dweller could set up barriers of sandbags, whether improvised from scavenged materials or actual canvas bags purchased ahead of time and stored for this purpose. Add in the likely plentiful old furniture and other detritus that can be scrounged from nearby homes and apartment buildings, and a fence that is almost impenetrable could be thrown together fairly quickly. Don't overlook the possibility of pushing or towing inoperable vehicles and using them as a base for your primary barrier.

Area Denial

Area denial is a concept where you try to reduce or eliminate the ability of your attackers to come to you through certain areas. In essence, you deny them access to specific parts of your perimeter.

Area denial comes into play through essentially two scenarios. The first is if you have a portion of your perimeter that is not easily kept under surveillance in the course of day-to-day activities. A blind spot like this would be a great place for an area denial system. The second scenario would involve funneling, where you try to move your attackers into an area you can more easily defend.

There are two types of area denial systems, lethal and non-lethal. Unless there are members of your group who are exceptionally experienced in handling explosives and other ordinance, and also have legal access to the requisite materials in order to safely stockpile them ahead of time, I suggest you concentrate on the non-lethal approach.

Remember the boxwood hedge we discussed in the barrier section? You can use it for area denial as well. In an urban or suburban area, simply making piles of rusted, broken metal and smashed wood will serve the same purpose. The idea is to make the area of your perimeter too difficult to easily cross, which forces the attackers to find another area that looks like an easier option.

BOOBY TRAP

One idea that falls into the category of area denial is what we might call a booby trap. For example, let's say you have a fence run on a blind side of your property. If you have the means to do so, consider digging a small trench that runs parallel to the fence. Place it about 3 feet from the inside of the fence. The ditch could be as small as 3 feet across and 2 feet deep. Line it with broken and rusty metal, boards with nails, and other surprises. In the dark, it won't be easily seen and someone climbing over the fence and jumping to the ground, or rushing to get through a hole they just made in the fence, will be in for an awakening. Granted, it may only work on the first one or two people coming in that way, but their shouts of surprise and pain will give away their position. This idea works even better if you have a way to conceal the ditch, turning it into a shallow punji pit.

Attackers may attempt to take advantage of some of your area denial measures by using them as cover or concealment. You can mitigate this risk by using booby traps. For example, scatter shards of broken glass on the ground behind your hedge. Cover the glass with leaves and it likely won't be noticed until the attacker crouches

---

COVER VERSUS CONCEALMENT

There is a big difference between the terms cover and concealment.

Cover will protect one from incoming fire. Examples would include thick walls, large trees, and boulders.

Concealment, on the other hand, just hides you but provides little or no protection. A hedge might provide excellent concealment but absolutely zero cover capability.

---

or lies down into it. Another option would be to use locations such as these for emptying your portable toilets.

THE LETHAL APPROACH

Should you decide to go with lethal options for area denial, you'll need to ensure that every single member of your team knows exactly where the devices are, so as to prevent any accidents.

I will make mention of one possible option to explore for a lethal area denial device. I have reason to believe that if you were to take a small perfume bottle, about the size of a golf ball, and fill it with black powder, then detonate it with the current from a lantern battery, it would be powerful enough to basically vaporize a wooden mailbox. Obviously, implementing a device that potent is not something to do in a casual manner.

Alarms and Surveillance Systems

Bearing in mind that one of the primary purposes of securing the perimeter is to buy you time to engage and

FUNNELING

The purpose of funneling is simple. You want to drive your attackers into an area where you have a clear line of fire. With a combination of obstacles, area denial, and funneling, you can maintain control of the situation. This is also where a bit of psychology can come into play.

Take a good, hard look at your retreat location. Where do you want your attackers to be? Don't limit it to a single location; pick a few spots where the majority of your team will be have a clear view. Perhaps your driveway, the front lawn, or the courtyard in front of your apartment building would be good. Once you have those kill zones determined, think about how an attacker would approach your home. Do a 360-degree rotation and consider all angles.

Here's a sample scenario to illustrate how funneling works. Let's say if an attacking force were coming in from the south, they'd probably first crouch behind the hedge running along that side of the property. Spoil this option through the use of area denial measures.

Leaving that location in a hurry, the attackers will go left or right. Most people will, when given a choice, take the path that looks easier. If you want to funnel them closer to the driveway, then make the path going in the opposite direction look more difficult. Brush or piles of garbage will do the trick. Don't use something that would provide cover, as you don't want to offer them any sort of protection.

Keep them moving along by spoiling each possible cover or concealment location through the use of additional area denial measures. Once the bulk of the attackers have reached your chosen kill zone, take whatever action you deem necessary.

defeat an enemy, it makes sense to put into place various devices that will alert you to an attacker's presence. Alarms that rely on electricity to function may work in the short term but without a reliable means to power them, they will end up being not much more than interesting decoration. That doesn't mean you should discount their use totally, though. Just bear in mind that you'll need both electronic and manual means of detecting intruders.

Various types of alarm and surveillance systems can be had rather cheaply today and prices continue to drop. Many of the camera-based systems are sold with three or four cameras, plus a digital recorder. You simply provide a small monitor to observe the activity. Most of the cameras sold for this purpose are wireless, so there's no need to string coaxial cable all over the place. However, the signal transmitted by the cameras often isn't all that strong, so you'll need to experiment a bit to determine the actual range available to you. If you were to place a camera at the end of your driveway and also install a laser beam alarm, something commonly available at commercial electronics stores as well as many of the warehouse outlets like Sam's Club, you could quickly determine whether it was a deer or an intruder coming in your direction.

In an urban area, you could place early-warning devices in the buildings adjacent to yours. Put them just inside doors and ground level windows and you'll be warned if attackers attempt to set up shop in those buildings prior to coming for you. These devices could be as complex as covert cameras or as simple as trip wires tied to tin cans with pebbles inside. Use what is available to you. The important thing is to prevent blind sides to your defense.

Personally, I like what we can call silent alarms. By that, I mean an alarm that will sound on a separate receiver, rather than where the breach was made. This gives you an opportunity to be aware of an intruder without their knowing you've been alerted to their presence. This also helps to prevent anyone who has your area under surveillance from knowing where the tripwires and other devices are if they are tripped accidentally by wildlife, for example.

TRIPWIRES

There are a few DIY approaches to these alarm systems, at least in terms of how the alarms get tripped. One method uses just a simple spring clothespin. Connect the wires running from your alarm device to the jaws of the clothespin. Place a small piece of plastic between the jaws, preventing the wires from touching. A tripwire is connected to this piece of plastic and strung where you want to place the alarm. Then, when the tripwire is snagged, it pulls the plastic from the clothespin, causing the jaws to close, completing the electric circuit, and activating the alarm. This is a great low-tech approach for setting alarm systems. If you string this tripwire on the inside of your fence, a few inches from the top and several inches out, anyone attempting to climb over the fence will be detected.

Something to keep in mind about tripwires is that they can be easily detected if they are out in the open. Foiling a tripwire is usually just a simple matter of stepping over it. If you have an area where you wish to implement a tripwire, such as the space between two outbuildings, be sure to conceal it in some way. Run it through a bit of brush or something you can place on the ground. You'll want this concealment to be at least tall enough so someone can't easily step over it, but small enough that they

SNIPER TARGET SELECTION

If you have one or more members of your team acting in a sniper capacity, make sure that they're not just a good shot, but also know what to shoot at. One thing the sniper should concentrate on is taking out the leaders of an invading force. By losing their leadership, they will likely lose cohesion in their attack, suffering confusion and a sudden lack of morale and confidence.

Typically, the group leader will be located in the middle of the force, in what he or she believes is a well-protected location. The leader will not be the first person over the wall.

The leader will need to direct the actions of those he or she commands. This means that some form of communication will need to be in place. You might see someone with their ear to a radio frequently, or you might see several "runners" coming and going from the leader's location. Look for the person who seems to be doing the most talking.

In a formally organized group, the leader is often at least a bit older than those he or she commands, usually having advanced up the chain of command over a period of several years. In a post-collapse world, though, this may not be the case, so there is no guarantee that targeting the older members of the attacking group will net the leader.

may feel safe in moving it to the side, a movement which will activate the alarm.

LOOKOUT/SNIPER AND SPOTTER

On top of any gadgetry you implement, you should have lookouts posted if you can. Position them where they have as wide a view as possible and provide them with a way to communicate any possible threats to the rest of the team. Ideally, your lookout will also be adept at long-range shooting and will act as a sniper as needed.

If your resources allow for it, make sure you pair the lookout/sniper with a spotter. For our purposes, that

DIVERSION AND DECEPTION

Probably the most common attack strategy you'll face is the diversion. It comes in many forms and many of you have probably done some form of it at one time or another, perhaps when playing army as kids.

The basic idea is while your target is dealing with some distraction, you send in a group to attack from the side or rear. For example, a small group engages the target at the front gate or from the driveway. They call attention to themselves in some way, perhaps acting as a family who is just looking for a little food. While the personnel inside are handling that situation, a secondary force creeps in from the rear and hopefully takes the target by surprise.

As the potential target, upon seeing anyone coming down the driveway or attempting to enter the perimeter, no matter how innocent they appear, you should do everything you can to keep eyes out in all directions. Be wary of any sort of distraction or diversion.

person's job is first and foremost to protect the sniper. While the sniper is concentrating on taking out the opposing force's leadership, the spotter is keeping eyes closer to home and making sure no one is sneaking up on the sniper post. In a military capacity, the spotter would also be watching the shots taken by the sniper and helping him or her adjust their aim as needed. However, in a post-collapse world, it is doubtful your sniper will be taking the 600-yard shots that may necessitate a second set of eyes.

Keep in mind that the lookout/sniper position need not necessarily be within your perimeter. If there is a

Even the most innocent of appearances may be deceiving. Picture this—it is about four months after society has essentially crumbled. You and your family have settled into a routine of sorts and are getting by. One day, a small boy and girl come walking to your perimeter. They are disheveled, dirty, and very thin. It is hard to say for sure due to all the grime but they look to be maybe nine or ten years old. What do you do? Sure, you feel bad for them. And given the state of the country, they might very well be legit. But, they may also be there to feel out your defenses, to see how close they can get before being stopped. Heck, they might be armed or carrying a bomb.

Your best bet in that situation is to stop them well beyond your perimeter if at all possible. Give them directions to where they might find help, if such a location is known. If you are for some reason absolutely compelled to provide such individuals with assistance, do so at your own risk.

vacant apartment building across from you, having a lookout up on the fourth or fifth floor will give them a great vantage point. In a rural area, a position on a high hill overlooking the retreat will do nicely.

Planning Ahead

The final component of perimeter defense is to plan ahead of time how you will respond to alarms and other alerts. When an alarm sounds, you don't want your team to run around aimlessly, shouting at each other. Rather, you want them to respond quickly, efficiently, and fluidly.

Naturally, part of this planning is contingent on the resources available to you. A retreat with a couple dozen members will be able to respond in a much different fashion than a family of four. In any event, though, planning is key. Each member of your team should have clear-cut responsibilities during an intrusion response. These roles will need to be discussed in detail and drilled until they become automatic.

IDENTIFY THE THREAT

If the alarm is in a location where you cannot immediately determine who or what triggered it, identifying the potential threat will take priority. As part of your response planning, determine safe locations from which you will be able to observe every possible point of breach. For example, you might decide that if the alarm for the point behind the shed is tripped, a member of your team should immediately proceed to the rearmost southern window to take a peek.

No matter which of the early warning devices is activated, one of the first response actions should be having your long-range shooter or sniper get into position, assuming he or she isn't already there. They should report in immediately upon reaching their position and begin informing the team of what they are able to determine about the threat.

STAY IN COMMUNICATION

As we'll discuss in the chapter on communications, it is vitally important that your team have a way to keep each other appraised of the situation. Providing them with small handheld radios will be extremely beneficial. Whoever identifies the threat should immediately inform all members of the team so appropriate actions can be taken.

If the alarm and subsequent response alert you that an attack is indeed imminent or in progress, swift and decisive action may yet save the day.

CHAPTER 4
Structure Hardening

The term "structure hardening" refers to the measures taken to prevent forcible entry into a home or other building. While no structure can really be made completely impregnable, at least not through the means available to the average person, in this chapter we'll discuss various ways you can greatly increase the time and effort it would take ne'er-do-wells to get into your home. Remember, the primary purpose behind implementing security measures is not to completely prevent access, but rather to give you enough time to take action against intruders.

Structure hardening focuses on the three primary ways in which a home can be entered: doors, windows, and walls.

Doors

The strength of a door is measured in two ways. The first is the material of which the door is made. A cheap, hollow core interior door won't withstand much more than a simple kick before it splinters. A solid wood exterior door will hold up to more abuse, but if half the door is glass-paneled, how hard do you think it will be to break into? A steel-encased door would be ideal, but few people would want to install one, due to aesthetics as well as expense. So in most cases your best choice is a solid wood door with no windows of any kind.

The second way in which the strength of a door is measured is how many points of attachment it has. The more places the door is attached to the frame, the stronger it will be. At a minimum, the door should have three hinges, a locking doorknob, and a dead bolt. This gives you five points of attachment. An additional dead bolt toward the top of the door and another at the bottom will provide additional support against brute force entry.

HINGES

Most hinges are sold with very small screws meant to be used to attach the door to the frame. Get rid of those and purchase screws long enough to go through the doorframe and into the stud. This provides quite a bit of added strength.

With most hinges, it is a very simple matter to take out the hinge pins, allowing the door to be removed. For this reason, whenever possible you should install hinges on the interior side of the door.

STOP MOLDING

The stop molding is the strip of wood that runs the height of the door and prevents it from swinging too far. When you slam a door shut, this is the piece of wood the door hits, causing that satisfying "wham." If the stop molding

ANSWERING THE DOOR, POST-COLLAPSE

Bearing in mind that visits from door-to door-salespeople and Jehovah's Witnesses are probably going to be few and far between after a societal collapse, for your own safety you'll need to change how you answer knocks on the door. This applies particularly to those who find themselves in a situation where they've not been able to implement much of a perimeter, allowing strangers access to the front door itself.

Should there come a knock on the door, under no circumstances should you step to the door and inquire as to the identity of the visitor. A relatively common intrusion technique in war-torn areas is, once the visitor hears someone answer from the other side of the door, he or she sends a few bullets through the door, injuring or killing the person inside. The door is then kicked open and the intruders are inside, making what was probably already a bad day much, much worse.

is accessible from the outside of the door, it could be pried up, allowing access to the bolts and locks. Given that these moldings are typically just tacked in place with small nails, that is not too difficult to accomplish. The way doors are usually installed, either the hinges or the stop molding will be accessible to someone outside.

For better security, remove the stop moldings, take out the nails, and reinstall the molding using wood glue and longer nails. If the nails you are using are considerably thicker than the ones previously used, you may want to drill pilot holes in order to avoid cracking or splintering the molding.

Find a location within the home where you can observe the outside of the front door. This could be a side window or a room upstairs. Then when a visitor appears, without verbally acknowledging them, you can peep and see who it is. If you determine that it is someone who shouldn't be knocking on your door, you can take whatever action you deem appropriate.

While using a peephole in the door without making any noise seems like a good idea, I can tell you from years of professional experience that it is quite easy to see if someone is looking through the peephole. If I'm outside and see the peephole suddenly darken, I can surmise there is an eyeball on the other side. Further, someone on the outside can see movement inside the home, even if they can't determine exact details. If you absolutely must use a peephole, you can mitigate this somewhat by covering it with a dark cloth.

DEAD BOLTS

Whether you go with one or several dead bolts, they are rather simple to install. The hardest part can be determining exactly where the strike boxes should be installed. (The strike box is the metal box that is installed into the doorframe; this is what the bolt slides into when the dead bolt is locked.) A simple way to do this is to take a tube of old lipstick and color the end of the bolt. Then, when the door is closed, snap the dead bolt so the bolt comes out and pushes against the frame. Open the door and you'll see exactly where the strike box should be located.

Again, all screws should be long enough to go through the frame and into the stud.

DOORKNOBS

Honestly, the doorknob, locked or not, provides so little protection overall that it really doesn't matter a whole lot which kind you install. Just make sure it is installed correctly and is tight and secure, rather than rattling loosely in the door.

FIRE VECTORS

As with all our other defenses, we plan for the worst-case scenario. With regard to structure hardening, this would be someone gaining access to the home. This is where fire vectors come into play. Determine every point of possible entry, then figure out where you can be positioned in a place of cover and still be able to get a bead on the intruder.

For example, let's say there is an exterior door in the kitchen. If you are able to see this door, or at least the majority of the kitchen, from a position around the corner and down the hallway, this would be where you'd place a sandbag barrier. Should someone come through that door, you can be positioned behind the sandbags and dispatch the intruder.

Plan these fire vectors throughout the home. Whenever possible, determine several "safe" positions for each possible point of entry, including all interior rooms. Even if your living room is completely isolated from points of exterior entry, plan for someone making it that far into the home.

SAWPROOFING

Aside from just kicking in the door, another way intruders may try to gain access is to saw through the door around the dead bolts and doorknob. This can be accomplished quickly if an electric "Sawzall" is available, marginally slower if done manually. You can prevent this by installing metal rods into the solid wood door. This requires the use of an electric drill, a 12-inch thin bit, a hammer, a nail set, and ¼-inch unthreaded steel rods 7 or 8 inches long.

Drill holes in the edge of the lock side of the door. Space them such that you have a couple of them above and below every dead bolt and the doorknob. The holes should be deep enough to contain the steel rods with about ½-inch of additional space. Once the holes are drilled, drive the steel rods into the door and use the nail set to drive them past the edge of the door. Fill the remaining bit with wood putty.

You can further strengthen the door by installing one or more removable bars across the inside. You've probably seen this concept in any number of movies set in the Old West. Affix metal brackets on either side of the doorframe, using long screws or lag bolts to go into the studs. Then, lay a 2x4 or other thick piece of wood into the brackets. Of course, this only works on doors that open to the interior. This method is an excellent option for those who live in apartments or other rental properties where the landlord would probably frown on someone installing additional dead bolts and such. Just purchase the materials, including a cordless drill, drill bits, and screws, and have it all sitting in a closet for when it may be needed. The brackets can be screwed to the walls in a matter of minutes. Be sure though to keep the cordless drill charging at all times so you don't find the battery dead when you need it.

PATIO DOORS

These sliding doors can be something of a nightmare in terms of security. Most homeowners know the trick of laying a wooden dowel in the track at the bottom of the door, preventing the door from sliding open. This does work reasonably well, provided the intruder has a reason to not just smash through the glass. Replacing the glass with shatter-resistant plastic will help eliminate that option.

DIY SANDBAGS

Sandbags provide excellent protection against firearms because they pack a great deal of mass into a small package. The mass stops the force of the bullet. Sandbags generally work much better than other barriers like metal sheeting because the bullet isn't sent ricocheting around the room.

Despite the name, you need not necessarily use sand. Dirt, kitty litter, and clay are all options that work just as well. You can purchase empty sandbags at many home improvement stores, particularly if you're located in an area that experiences flooding on a regular basis. If you can't find them at local stores, they are also available online. You can find sandbags made of plastic or cloth and either will work for our purposes. If filling material is a concern, shop garden store clearance sales at the end of summer and pick up bags

With a little effort you can find special bar locks and dead bolts that are made specifically for sliding doors. These generally work very well and are a great option to explore.

GARAGE DOORS

Garage doors typically come with a bar lock preinstalled. These work very well in preventing the door from opening. If for some reason the lock itself doesn't work, the doors generally have a sliding latch as well. A flat piece of metal, it slides through a hole in the track, stopping the door from moving up. Often this latch will come with

of cheap soil. You could even just skip the sandbags and use these bags of dirt.

Fill the bags only about halfway to prevent them from becoming too heavy. They should weigh about 30 to 40 pounds each. You can either tie them shut using rope or just fold the top over underneath the bag when you set it in place.

Stack them in walls no more than three or four high to prevent them from toppling. This also keeps the overall weight down. Because they are so heavy, I'd avoid using them in any large quantity in upper levels of the home. Let's say you use forty sandbags in one area, that's somewhere in the neighborhood of 1,200 to 1,600 pounds; not every floor can withstand that kind of weight.

Placing stacks of sandbags in various locations around the home will provide you with relatively safe locations for returning fire.

a hole on the end where you can place a padlock. This prevents the latch from being slid open.

Windows

Windows generally prove to be not much of a deterrent to an intruder. Any parent of a child who loves playing baseball is well aware of how easy it can be to break a window. This can be mitigated by replacing the glass with shatter-resistant plastic. Sold under brand names like Lexan, it is strong enough to withstand blows with a hammer. You can buy it in sheets and cut it to size using a circular saw with a plywood finishing blade or a jigsaw with a metal cutting blade. Go slow to avoid chipping.

Absent being able to smash through the glass, an intruder will have to somehow force the window open. For double-hung windows, this can be prevented simply by drilling a hole through the window sashes and sliding a nail slightly smaller in diameter into the hole. The hole should go at least ½-inch into the bottom rail of the top sash. You want the hole a bit larger than the nail so you can easily remove the nail to open the window as needed. Angle the hole downward so the nail won't just fall out on its own. Do this twice for each window, about 2 inches from either side.

Horizontal sliding windows can be secured like sliding doors as mentioned earlier. Casement windows are tricky but generally they are very difficult to open from the outside to begin with (and in my house, almost impossible to open from the inside as well!). However, for added security, you can add special latches that require the use of a key to open.

One key thing to remember when it comes to securing windows is that by installing any of these various measures, you are not only preventing access from the outside, but also possibly trapping yourself and your family inside in the event of a fire. If you are considering installing permanent security measures such as the window grilles we're about to discuss, weigh this carefully against the potential need for rapid escape.

WINDOW GRILLES

While not the prettiest things in the world, bars installed over windows will certainly deny access to most intruders. However, these can be difficult for the average person to install correctly. The grilles should be anchored to the most solid part of the wall available. Use strong lag bolts for this rather than wood screws, if at all possible. Once the grille is installed, go back to the lag bolts and use a handheld grinder to round off the heads, making them all but impossible to remove. If you're forced to use wood screws, use the grinder to deface the heads enough so a screwdriver won't be able to engage the screw head.

Walls

While doors and windows may provide convenient openings through which an intruder can enter the home, the walls in most stick-built homes are not all that difficult to breach. If the home has simple vinyl siding over pressboard, a few minutes with a chainsaw or even a sledge-

SECURING OUTBUILDINGS

If you have sheds, barns, or other types of outbuildings on your property, you need to make sure those are secured, for several reasons. First, the contents of these outbuildings would be vulnerable to theft if not secured. Second, the tools and equipment inside could be used to facilitate entry into the main home (maybe you have a chainsaw in there that an intruder would find all too handy). Third, unsecured outbuildings provide concealment and possibly cover for the attackers.

Secure these outbuildings using the same techniques as the main home, paying particular attention to the typically flimsy doors and windows used on sheds and barns. You should also install some form of early warning device to alert you to intrusion attempts. This could be as simple as a tripwire-activated alarm.

hammer would be all it would take to create a new door. With that said, though, it would take a rather determined intruder to go that route. Most people are conditioned to focus on doors and windows to gain entry.

If your budget is sufficiently high, brick exterior walls provide a considerable increase in wall strength. However, even these can be defeated by a sufficiently motivated intruder armed with a sledgehammer and a bit of time.

Interior walls in most homes provide just about zero protection against firearms. Remember what we said about cover versus concealment? Interior walls provide great concealment but no cover, though the cover element can be improved with sandbags and other mass-heavy items.

CHAPTER 5

Safe Rooms

The use of safe rooms dates back to the Middle Ages. Castle "keeps" were built deep within the castle as places where the royals could hide during a siege. Going forward in history, this type of special hidden room was used to hide slaves escaping through the Underground Railroad as well as later to hide booze during Prohibition. Storm cellars are also a type of safe room, protecting the residents during tornadoes.

The modern safe room is something of an offshoot of the old bomb shelters from the mid-1900s. Those shelters, usually built underground, were designed to protect families in the event of a nuclear attack. Searching online, you can find copies of the old Civil Defense plans for building bomb shelters. Some were fairly elaborate, incorporating multiple rooms as well as ventilation systems.

Today, safe rooms have become very popular among society's elite—actors, politicians, and wealthy industrialists for example. Fearing everything from kidnapping to riots, many of these very well-to-do individuals have had customized panic rooms installed in or under their mansions. Costing upwards of six digits, these luxurious safe rooms have every modern convenience as well as extensive surveillance systems and remote alarm capabilities.

Here's the thing though. Safe rooms like these are based on one underlying principle. At some point after entering the safe room, the cavalry will arrive in the form of armed officers riding in squad cars. The safe room will serve its purpose by protecting the individuals and their families for a few hours at the most while they wait for the boys in blue. In a post-collapse world, there is no cavalry coming to save the day. In a world without the rule of law, it will just be a waiting game where the aggressors are confident in knowing at some point you'll run out of water or food, stick your head out, and they'll be there to greet you. While they wait, they'll have free reign of the rest of the home and avail themselves of all your carefully stockpiled supplies. If they get really antsy, they have all the time in the world to work on breaking down the door, at which point it will be like shooting ducks in a barrel.

Now, with all that said, installing a safe room in your home or retreat isn't the worst possible idea. It will provide a measure of safety and security in disasters that don't involve armed hordes knocking down your door. For example, if there were a major weather-related crisis, a safe room would naturally give you and your family a great place to ride it out. It could also be a rallying point for your group, a place where they could hole up and refocus their efforts on repelling aggressors.

Planning the Safe Room

For our purposes here, we'll focus on building a safe room from scratch. The reason for this is it is far easier to include the necessary features when you are building from the ground up. However, many necessities could be added to an existing room so don't discount this option completely.

The size of your safe room should be contingent upon how many people it is designed to hold. For emergencies of short duration, such as a tornado, you should allot at least 5 square feet of floor space per person. Notice I said square feet of floor space, not overall room size. As we'll discuss later, you'll want to stock some supplies in the safe room and that space needs to be accounted for as well. Five square feet per person is the absolute minimum and if you plan to occupy the safe room for longer than perhaps an hour or two, that space needs to be increased dramatically. Planning for occupancy of twenty-four hours or greater will require at least 7 or 8 square feet per person. Why? So you and your family members have enough space to lie down comfortably. So, if you have a family of five and plan to stay in the safe room for up to three days, you'd need a minimum floor size of 35 to 40 square feet, not counting the space your supplies will take up. This still isn't a lot of space in the safe room but while you want to keep comfort in mind to a degree, you're not building it as a weekend getaway either. Adding in extra space for gear and supplies, the family of five could probably get away with a room that is 7 feet square.

SAFE ROOM DOS AND DON'TS
by Laurie Neverman

Like any aspect of preparedness, safe rooms are only as good as the planning and products that go into them. Cut corners, and they may fail you when you need them most.

Build your room to address the seismic, weather, and other potential hazards you are likely to face in your area. Look at every aspect of the room, including the entrance—a weak door is a fail point. A strong door in a weak frame is a fail point. I think most of us have seen tornado and hurricane debris driven through tree trunks and appliances—a standard lightweight door is not going to cut it. Make sure the door opens in, not out, in case debris blocks the exit.

Proper crossbracing/reinforcement in the walls and ceiling is essential. A safe room that collapses under load (winds, building collapse, etc.) is nothing more than a death trap. Do some research before you build—don't be that guy who just starts digging a hole in the backyard, only to run into a high water table or unstable earth. Don't think you can just bury any old container in the yard and call it good. Soil is heavy, and wet soil is even heavier.

Whether your safe room is at or below ground level, make sure it is securely tied to a foundation. You don't want to have a projectile-proof door and walls only to have the entire structure tear loose.

Generally speaking, in most cases the ideal location for a safe room is in the basement. Placing it here provides a great level of security against Mother Nature's wrath. Assuming, of course, your home isn't build it an area prone to flooding, that is. If that's the case, then you'll

Make sure you have a source of fresh air. My entire home is made from insulated concrete forms (ICFs), a popular choice for safe rooms, and I can guarantee that it gets a little stuffy inside when the doors and windows are closed. Now imagine—small room, several people, possibly pets, emergency supplies, panicked breathing—and no fresh air. You get the picture.

Think about who and what is going to be in that room. Will you have enough room for your entire family? Will others be allowed inside? What about pets? Which critical supplies stay in the room, which are placed nearby in hopes that you will be able to reach them if needed? Water, food, blankets, lighting, communication, medicine, valuables, ammo, some items for the kids—where are your priorities?

My husband is ex-military, and he likes to cite the "7 Ps"— "Proper Prior Planning Prevents Piss Poor Performance." Know your risks, plan appropriately, and stay safe when it counts.

Laurie Neverman has a BS in Math/Physics and an MS in Mechanical Engineering with an emphasis in renewable energy. She and her family live in the upper Midwest in an environmentally friendly/energy efficient/accessible/newfangled/old-fashioned home with solar panels, a root cellar, and an herbal apothecary. She is a homeschooling, homesteading mother with a passion for natural healing, gardening, and ancient history. You can connect with her at www.CommonSenseHome.com.

want to go a bit higher. However, with all that said, the downside is if you intend to use the safe room as protection against some sort of bandit horde, a basement is probably the worst place to be. Unless, of course, you plan ahead and provide for some sort of last resort escape route. I don't advise building any sort of underground tunnel though unless you truly know what you're doing. Otherwise, you may just be building nothing more than a mass grave.

Safe Room Construction

If you plan to use one or more of your home's existing walls as part of your safe room, they will need to be reinforced. FEMA suggests all walls of a safe room contain steel reinforcement to protect against missiles sent flying by tornados or hurricanes. Further, the ceiling of the safe room should be reinforced as well and built separate from the ceiling of the basement or other room in which the safe room is constructed.

One of the easiest ways to build a safe room is to start with doubled up 2x4 studs for the walls. The outer side of the studs should then be covered by steel plating, then two layers of ½-inch or ¾-inch plywood with the grain oriented in opposite directions. The doubled studs will be needed due to the weight of the steel and plywood. You can then cover the plywood with drywall for aesthetics. The ceiling will be constructed in a similar manner but with doubled 2x6 joists taking the place of the studs, of course.

Naturally, if you're building the safe room in the basement and you plan to place it in a corner, it'll be difficult to place the steel and plywood on the outside of the studs that lay against the existing basement walls. That's OK, just put the steel and plywood on the inside of those studs but bear in mind you'll probably have to add furring strips to the steel if you want to attach drywall to make things look nicer. Same thing applies to the ceiling of your safe room.

Add a steel door with a steel frame. It makes little sense to build these heavy-duty walls and then install a cheap, hollow door. Don't worry too much about a locking door knob, just go straight to installing two or three heavy-duty dead bolts. You want a door that will be almost impossible for the average attacker to hammer down.

Stocking the Safe Room

Now, given that you may need this safe room as a storm shelter or to barricade you and your family against home invasions *before* there is some sort of catastrophic collapse, make sure you have a landline telephone wired into the room, as well as electrical power. Without power, it'll be mighty dark in there. If you do end up calling the police from inside the safe room, be sure to explain to the dispatcher where the safe room is located within your home so the responding officers know where to look.

Given that you have no accurate way of determining how long you and your family may be holed up in the safe room after a natural disaster, plan for at least a few days. Food, water, flashlights, blankets and pillows, maybe a few things to help pass the time like decks of cards or books. A couple battery powered fans would be great as while the safe room won't be completely air tight, it will get stuffy after a while.

As I alluded to at the outset of this chapter, please do not take the inclusion of the information on safe rooms to mean I wholeheartedly support their use in a post-collapse world. In most situations I can envision occurring in a world without the rule of law, I believe safe rooms would become nothing more than convenient death traps. But, given their popularity today, I felt it incumbent upon myself to include the information so that families are better prepared for the more run of the mill disasters.

CHAPTER 6
Secure and Hidden Storage

Most of us, when we were kids, had at least one or two hiding spots for our goodies. Maybe between the mattress and box spring, maybe at the back of a shelf closet, perhaps someplace a bit more ingenious. I knew one classmate who used an air vent near his bed to hide magazines he had "borrowed" from his old man.

Look for places in your home that can provide secure and hidden storage, especially those that take advantage of idiosyncrasies of the structure that only you are aware of. Then if undesirables do get into your home, you will be able to keep your supplies and weapons safe from them, at least in the short term. This will not only help you avoid losing your stuff, but also assist you in fighting back.

Devising methods of hidden storage can certainly be a fun exercise too. It is an area of preparedness where you can truly be creative and think outside the box. I'm sure after reading through the following suggestions you'll be able to come up with your own ideas as well. We'll start in the basement and work our way up, also taking time to discuss the option of caching offsite.

The Basement

The basement offers a number of promising options for hidden storage, including pipes, air ducts, and drop ceilings, as well as boxes that may already be there.

PIPES

If you go into your basement and look up, you'll likely see at least a few large outflow pipes for your wastewater system. One more run of matching PVC pipe would not look at all out of place and would be roomy enough inside to hide a slim rifle, as well as many other valuable supplies.

Hang the pipe so it looks as though it joins up with an existing run and make sure it is hung securely, keeping in mind the weight it may have to hold. Take a good look at how the existing pipe is hung and whenever possible use the same type of hangers so everything matches in appearance. Cap off the open end of the pipe but don't use sealant; just tighten the cap by hand so you can open it quickly when you need to do so.

DIVERSION SAFES

There are many different items manufactured today designed for hiding valuables in plain sight. Called diversion safes, these include various canned products like shaving cream and hairspray as well as clocks, books, and even flower pots. For our purposes, most of these would work well as long as you avoid the diversion safes made to look like food products. If your home were to be raided, the people breaking in would probably be looking for food and would almost certainly snatch up any canned fruit and jars of peanut butter they see. Sure, they'd be in for a surprise later when they open the jar and find a brick of .22 shells, but I doubt they'd be all that disappointed.

AIR DUCTS AND DROP CEILINGS

Exposed air ducts can also be used to hide things. Take off one of the vents by removing the screws and place your items inside. When you replace the vent, leave the screws loose enough that you can undo them by hand. However, avoid blocking the entire duct; you don't want to impede the airflow to a great degree. Also avoid using this method to store items that will be affected by extremes of heat and cold.

If you have a drop ceiling in your finished basement, take down a couple of the ceiling panels and see what's behind them. Odds are if you hunt around a bit, you'll find a suitable location for placing a shelf on the side of one of the joists. This would be a great place for canned goods, a handgun or two, or ammo.

BOXES

In many homes, the basement is the storage area, filled with boxes of clothes, books, and other accumulations. Use this to your advantage and stash items in boxes, then cover the items with old clothes. Label the box something like "Grandma's delicates" and seal it up.

You can make things easier on yourself in terms of organization by using the same sort of label for every box that actually contains supplies. Scatter them throughout the storage area to make it look more realistic. Pay attention to the weight of the boxes, though. If you label the box as though it contains clothing, and hide several boxes of ammo inside, the weight might be a clue that the box is hiding something.

The Main Level

Moving up to the main level of your home, hidden storage options include doors, closets, and interior walls.

DOORS

One great place to hide small valuables is inside a door. If you have a solid wood interior door, say for a bedroom, take it off the hinges and out to the garage. Bore a small hole in the top edge of the door using a drill or chisel, being careful that you don't get too close to the edges of the door and splinter it all apart. Only go a couple inches down into the door; any more than that and you're just asking for something to go awry. When you're finished, put the door back up. You can use that hole to hide small things like the key to your gun safe. Put in the key, pad it with some cotton so it doesn't rattle around, and it will take a pretty darn thorough search to find it.

CLOSETS

Most closets have empty space on the inside above the door. While a shelf installed there isn't truly hidden, most searchers will overlook that area. You can also build a false wall in the back of a closet. Unless you're handy enough to create a moveable wall, you won't be able to access this storage area without damaging it. But for long-term storage, it can be an ideal spot. Place your items in the back of the closet, then build a frame of 2x4 lumber in front of it. Cover it with drywall and paint to match the rest of the closet. If you do this right, only a very keen eye will be able to detect the change. To get at your goodies, cut or smash a hole in the drywall.

INTERIOR WALLS AND MOLDINGS

A similar approach will allow you to hide things right inside your interior walls. Move an existing bookcase away from the wall and cut a hole in the drywall a foot or so up from the floor. (Avoid doing this next to or above an outlet to prevent hitting conduit or wiring.) After hiding your stuff, you can either patch the hole with drywall and paint it to match or just leave it exposed and replace the bookcase. A third option is to plan ahead and cut the hole so it matches an air vent you've purchased. Cover the hole with the air vent and use nails instead of screws so it will quickly pull out from the wall for ease of access.

You can also hide items behind the molding that runs along the top of your walls. Carefully remove the molding and cut the drywall to open a storage space. Use a 2x4 to create a shelf between the studs, place your items on the shelf, and replace the molding. Of course, the larger the molding you have, the bigger the storage space available to you.

The Attic

The attic is much like the basement in that it often serves as a storage area for the home. However, in most homes it is subject to extremes of heat and cold, so keep that in mind as you plan out what you might want to store there. You can use the same box trick as you did in the basement. Another option, if you have exposed insulation along the bottom of the attic, is to just hide things inside the insulation. However, be careful with storing anything heavy this way; you don't want a case of canned peaches to come crashing down into the bedroom below.

Caches

A cache (pronounced like "cash," not "cashay") is a collection of items you have hidden somewhere, typically offsite. For our purposes here, the idea behind having hidden caches in the area is that if you are forced to evacuate your home or retreat empty-handed, you will at least have some supplies to fall back on. In the event that team members return home to find that the home has been seized, a cache can give them access to additional weaponry and ammunition with which to engage the enemy.

Caches are also sometimes placed along preplanned routes between work and home, or home and a fallback location, to be used as needed immediately after a catastrophic event. For example, say you are at the office and an EMP hits, forcing you to head home on foot. While you will hopefully have your get-home bag with you, caches along the way will allow you to resupply as needed.

HOW TO STORE YOUR CACHE

One of the best ways to build a cache is out of PVC. This is because PVC is very resistant to outside pressure. After you bury a cache, over time it will be subject to great amounts of pressure from the sides as the ground shifts and settles. A simple box will eventually be crushed. You could also use sealed ammo cases purchased from military surplus stores, as these are quite durable as well. But, for my money, I'll stick with PVC tube caches.

You can make cache tubes from any size PVC tube. Cut the tube into 4-foot sections (or less if you don't need them that long). Using pipe dope, affix a permanent end cap on one end of the tube and a threaded end cap on the other. Fill the tube with your supplies, then screw in the end cap plug. These screw-in plugs usually have a squared-off knob on the outside, allowing you to use a wrench to tighten and loosen the plug.

One thing to bear in mind is that the tube may be very difficult to open after being sealed in the ground for up to several years. To assist with opening the threaded plug, you might consider sealing a small adjustable wrench in several layers of plastic and burying it next to the tube.

An additional step some folks use when building these supply cache tubes is to actually seal a smaller-diameter tube inside the large tube. This is because it may prove very difficult to remove the large tube from the ground, due to the ground having settled around it. The idea is to just dig down enough to expose the threaded cap of the large tube, remove that plug, then reach inside and pull out the smaller tube that contains the supplies. Should you decide to go that route, do yourself a favor and affix a length of wire or cord to the top of the smaller tube, making an easy-to-grab handle.

WHAT TO INCLUDE

What should go into a survival cache? Properly treated with oil and preservative, firearms can be stored in this manner, remaining well hidden until needed. Be sure to include a good cleaning kit in the cache to remove the preservative later on.

In addition to firearms, you could store just about anything you'd normally have in a get-home bag, such as a fire-starting kit, first aid supplies, and water purification tablets. However, bear in mind that there is always the chance moisture could seep into the tube, so everything should be sealed in plastic prior to being placed inside.

LOCATION, LOCATION

Once your caches are assembled, the next step is to determine their location. Most caches are designed to be buried. If you'll be placing them on your own property, consider putting them near the boundary edges. It makes very little sense to bury a cache 5 feet from your home. The ideal would be placing them in such a location that someone digging it up wouldn't be visible from the home. If that means burying it on property that doesn't belong to you, tread very carefully. The authorities will take a dim view of you burying a large cylinder made of PVC on public property, especially when you're likely to be doing so in the middle of the night. Perhaps you can work out some agreement with a neighbor in the area, if you feel they would be amenable to such an arrangement.

If there is any chance at all that the area of your cache location may at some point be visited by one or more treasure hunters equipped with metal detectors, do yourself a favor and bury some metal junk several inches above the top of your cache tube. This will effectively camouflage your cache. When they get a "hit," they'll dig down and find those rusty bolts and such, causing them to give up and move on.

MARK WHERE THE CACHE IS HIDDEN

The importance of being able to find the exact location of your survival cache tube cannot be overemphasized. The cache does you absolutely no good whatsoever if you can't find it when you need it. One of the easiest methods is to memorize the location relative to natural landmarks—but bear in mind that these things can change over time. Trees can be cut down. Boulders could be relocated to the front of someone's McMansion. Always have at least three different locators in mind to find your cache. For example, fifty paces straight north from a particular oak tree, seventy-two paces east from that large boulder, and eighty-nine paces south from this fence post.

Another option is to create customized markers for the location. Purchase or find odd-shaped, natural-looking stepping stones and place one on top of each cache location. Of course, you'll still need to remember the general area of the cache, but using these stones will hopefully prevent you from digging in the wrong place.

URBAN CACHES

Of course, burying cache tubes may be difficult if not impossible in urban areas. One alternative cache location that immediately comes to mind would be one of those "U-Store-It" storage rental units. The rent on a small unit usually isn't too expensive and even if the disaster is truly dire, it will be quite some time, I think, before those places get looted. Practice good OPSEC, though, and stash your supplies inside falsely labeled boxes as we discussed earlier.

If you have a city park nearby, visit one of the restroom outbuildings there. You could possibly stash a supply cache above the drop ceiling there, though of course you do run the risk of it being discovered at some point during renovation or repair work. Another option at the park would be to visit with your family, bringing along a tent, ostensibly for the kids to play in while you're there. Planning ahead, you've cut a hole in the bottom of the tent. Once it is set up, you could go inside and dig the hole for your supply cache. You may have difficulty in disposing of the extra soil you've displaced, though, so plan accordingly.

Abandoned buildings are another idea but you'll need to monitor the location regularly to make sure it isn't demolished with your stuff inside. You also need to be very careful when exploring buildings like this, as they are not only unsafe for general walking through but often harbor all sorts of vermin, four-legged and otherwise.

Some people advocate renting lockers at bus stations and the like for storage options. Personally, I don't think those locations are the safest even when times are good, let alone in a situation where you'd truly need the cached supplies. Furthermore, you'd need to change lockers on a regular basis, as they are inspected and cleaned out fairly often.

DOWNSIZING

One way to effectively hide caches in an urban area is to downsize a bit first. Instead of looking for a hiding spot for a 4-foot PVC tube or a sealed 5-gallon bucket, look for a place to hide a 1-gallon plastic bag with food and a fire-starting kit inside. Attach it to a rock and sink it near the shore at park pond, for example. Or bury it near the base of a large tree just off the trail. Consider putting together several of these small caches and spreading them around a bit, rather than trying to hide the entire stash in one spot.

The final consideration when it comes to caches is this: Never cache something you can't afford to lose. You can never be absolutely sure your cache won't be destroyed during a renovation, discovered by someone geocaching, or rendered impossible to locate when a marking is obscured.

SECTION III

PREPPER ARMORY

CHAPTER 7
Firearms

For the most part, firearm selection is a very personal matter. You have to take into account factors such as the purpose of the firearm, the experience of the shooter, and the shooter's physical abilities or limitations. Buying a tricked-out Desert Eagle .44 magnum semiautomatic pistol for someone who is scarcely 5 feet tall, cracks 100 pounds only when soaking wet and holding a brick, and has wrists thinner than uncooked spaghetti is just asking for trouble. Sure, the pistol looks really cool and it'll put good sized holes in anything hit with it. But it just might fracture one of those wrists at the same time.

Firearms are tools, nothing more and nothing less. There is nothing inherently evil about guns. There may very well be evil intent behind the pistol or rifle, depending on who is holding it and where it gets pointed. But in and of itself a firearm is nothing but a collection of metal and plastic. It has no feelings nor is it self-aware. There have, however, been cases where the firearm apparently loaded itself when no one was looking, so please watch out for that as you clean and handle your weapons.

Basic Firearms

Many, if not most, experts would agree there are essentially four categories of firearms to consider for the prepper armory: the .22 caliber rifle, the shotgun, the hunting rifle, and the handgun. We'll consider the merits of each in the following sections.

.22 LONG-RIFLE RIMFIRE

For those who grow up in rural areas, this is often the first firearm they are taught to use. A good quality .22 rifle will provide many years of solid use. From a prepper's standpoint, it will fill the dinner pot with rabbit, squirrel, and other small game and serve well as a varmint gun.

The Ruger 10/22 rifle has become the standard by which most other .22 rifles are measured. The standard version has been around since about 1964 and has been

incredibly popular since it first came out. There are approximately a bazillion different aftermarket modifications and add-ons that have come out for it, but it'll do just fine right out of the box, so to speak.

One of the reasons the .22 rifle is popular among preppers is cost. As I write this, a Ruger 10/22 can be found, brand new, for right around 200 bucks. You can sometimes find them used for around half that if you keep your eyes open. Ammunition is also very inexpensive, with fifty-round boxes going for under two bucks. This means you can stock up on thousands of rounds for very little money. Plus, it doesn't cost you an arm and a leg to spend an afternoon at the range with it. You can send a few hundred rounds down the range for the cost of a fast food kid's meal.

Obviously, the .22 caliber rifle isn't the most powerful weapon, and as such it is not ideal as a primary defensive weapon. With that said, though, anyone who says you can't kill a person with a .22 caliber weapon is, quite simply, wrong.

SHOTGUN

Next up in the basic arsenal is the scattergun. There are few sounds more pucker-inducing than that of a shell being racked in a pump shotgun. That sound is almost universally recognized as being an "Oh crap" moment. This, coupled with the wide range of loads available, makes the shotgun ideal for home defense. Loaded with smaller shot, the shooter doesn't run as much risk of over-penetration as a rifle or handgun, where a bullet could go through the target as well as the wall behind it and strike a family member.

Shotguns are categorized by gauge, with the most common being 12-gauge. The gauge actually harkens back to the days of cannons. The number of the gauge is the fraction of a pound of lead that would fit into the barrel. Back in those days, a "12 pounder" cannon would hold a lead cannon ball weighing 12 pounds. So, a 12-gauge shotgun barrel will hold a lead ball weighing $\frac{1}{12}$ pound. By using this knowledge, we know a 10-gauge shotgun has a larger diameter barrel than a 12-gauge.

The 12-gauge is, as mentioned, the most popular size shotgun. As such, ammunition is extremely common and easily found almost everywhere. For defensive purposes, there are two basic types of shotgun shells—shotshells and slugs.

Shotshells are generally divided up between birdshot and buckshot. Birdshot shells contain dozens of small pellets about the size of Bbs. Realistically, for defensive purposes birdshot is only really suitable for interior use. By that, I mean you and your target are inside the home and at fairly close range.

The most common shotshell today is 12-gauge 00 buckshot. It is suitable both for large game hunting as well as defense. While there is some variation by manufacturer and such, 00 buckshot generally contains less than a dozen pellets, though they are considerably larger than the pellets found in birdshot. This is a powerful shell and is devastating at reasonably close ranges, such as under 50 yards.

SAFETY

You've probably heard this a thousand times but it still remains an absolute truth when handling firearms: Consider every firearm to be loaded at all times. As I mentioned earlier in this chapter, firearms have a nasty habit of loading themselves when no one is paying attention. Even if you just cleared the weapon yourself, handle the weapon as though it is fully loaded. Never point it at a person you do not intend to fire upon.

As the shot leaves the barrel of the shotgun, it begins to spread. How quickly it spreads is contingent upon many factors, with the largest being the length and diameter of the barrel. Some shotguns have what is called an adjustable choke. This choke allows you to narrow the barrel diameter slightly, which increases the effective range of the shot by keeping it in a tighter pattern for longer distances. You can get the same effect with other shotguns by swapping out barrels for this purpose.

Slugs, on the other hand, consist of just one large metal lump. They are often used for large game hunting. While they do considerable damage to the target, for home defense purposes you'll likely want to avoid using slugs, due both to the overpenetration issue mentioned earlier as well as the fact that shot shells spread out and there is a higher risk of hitting an unintended target.

The Remington 870 is the most popular shotgun in the world, and for good reason. It is used by military and police forces the world over because it is exceptionally reliable and dependable. It is a rugged weapon that will stand up to extreme weather conditions and rarely, if ever, fail. Another great thing about the Remington is that it has remained virtually unchanged since its introduction. What this means to the prepper is the barrel from your brand new Remington 870 will fit the one your grandpa bought many years ago. The Mossberg 500 is another well-regarded shotgun and priced perhaps a touch cheaper than the Remington.

HUNTING RIFLE

The hunting rifle is the distance weapon in the arsenal. Properly outfitted with a scope, a well-practiced shooter should be able to consistently hit targets well beyond a thousand yards. This will allow you to keep aggressors at a considerable distance from your home. However, that skill doesn't come overnight, nor does it arrive in a handy

WHITE DEATH

Simo Häyhä was a sniper for the Finnish Army during the Winter War (1939–1940). He used his rifle, a variant of the Russian Mosin Nagant, to set a record of 505 confirmed kills. Even more impressive is that he accomplished this in less than one hundred days, averaging five kills per day. He used no scope, preferring to stick with the open iron sights of the rifle. In temperatures down to −40°, he survived several counter-attacks by the Russians, who had nicknamed him "White Death." He left the war after being shot in the jaw by a Russian soldier. Despite horrific wounds, Häyhä made a full recovery.

little box that you just need to unpack after purchasing. It takes many hours of practice at the range.

An inexpensive, yet very reliable, long gun is the Mosin Nagant. Available from a wide range of sporting goods stores for under $100, it gives you a lot of gun for very little money. It fires the 7.62mmx54R round, which is very similar to the 30.06 many hunters know well, and has an effective range of about a thousand yards. Naturally, priced that inexpensively, the Mosin Nagant doesn't have a lot of bells and whistles, but it is dependable and built to last. Other hunting rounds that are worth looking at include the 30/30 and the .300 Winchester Magnum, the latter particularly popular with several law enforcement agencies.

Take a look at your situation, though, before you go out and purchase a long-distance rifle. If you are in an urban environment, you may never need to fire at a target a thousand yards away. Take into account the lines of sight you have available to you and plan accordingly. If you cannot see more than 75 yards in any direction, you may be better off investing the money in additional shotguns and such.

HANDGUN

This is the category of firearm where the survivalist can easily spend quite a bit of money. Handguns are certainly not cheap, at least not ones that are of decent quality and caliber. This is also an area where the prepper really needs to shop around and make a carefully calculated decision. Many gun shops will rent handguns for customers to "test drive" before purchasing. If you have a local shop that offers this, I highly encourage you to take full advantage of it. Given that even a basic revolver can cost in excess of several hundred dollars, this will be an expensive, though necessary, purchase.

A handgun is by its very nature much more portable than a shotgun or rifle. It is easier to go about daily chores and tasks with a handgun on your hip than it is to do so while carrying a heavy shotgun. Considering that in a post-collapse situation there might be a lengthy period of time where you will want to be armed at all times, this is important.

One key decision that you will need to make when choosing a handgun is revolver or semiautomatic. For someone very new to handguns, I typically suggest they start with revolvers. They are less complicated, with fewer moving parts. They also don't jam. If a shell doesn't fire, you just pull the trigger again.

The largest advantage a semiautomatic has over a revolver is the capacity. Most revolvers carry six rounds in a cylinder. Semiautomatics use a magazine feed and can carry anywhere from eight to sixteen or more, depending on the caliber and type of magazine. Naturally, the more rounds available to the shooter before needing to reload, the better. But it won't matter how many rounds are in the magazine or cylinder if the shooter can't hit his target.

Worth considering though is the fact that with the higher capacity, a semiautomatic also requires a bit more maintenance. There are more moving parts involved as compared to a revolver. If you are the type of person who

PRACTICE

No one gets to be anything approaching competent with a firearm by letting it sit in a gun safe for months on end. It takes diligent practice, especially when just starting out, to become at least marginally proficient. Each and every firearm is unique and it can take some time to get used to the idiosyncrasies of each one. That absolutely will not happen without spending some time at the range.

Popping rounds at a stationary paper target is a great start but remember, when you'll need to shoot for real, the target probably won't be standing still. If you can arrange to do so somehow, practice firing at moving targets. Skeet shooting is one way to accomplish this.

Practice shooting from a variety of stances, including crouching and lying down. Don't forget to practice using your off-hand too. You might end up in a situation where your dominant hand is injured and you'll need to pull off a shot or two with your other wing.

has trouble with doing repairs on anything mechanical, you may be better off with a wheel gun.

The most common calibers for semiautomatic handguns include .45, .40, and 9mm. Any of these calibers is well suited for defense purposes. Another one worthy of consideration is .380, which is similar in size to the 9mm round. Ruger in particular has come out with some great handguns that use this round. I suggest you avoid the .44 magnum and larger rounds, whether you're talking semiauto or revolver. It is just too heavy and, to be honest, too much gun for the average prepper.

Another handgun worth considering for home defense is the Taurus Judge. This is a unique revolver that fires both .410 shotgun shells and .45 bullets. Loaded with birdshot, it poses little risk of penetrating walls if the shot misses the target, yet a hit will cause quite a bit of disabling pain.

When we talk about revolvers, there are two kinds—single action and double action. With a single action, the hammer must be manually pulled back before each shot may be fired. A double action has a longer trigger pull, the beginning of which cocks the hammer. For any circumstance that comes to my mind, a double action is going to be preferred over the single action.

In my opinion, if you are looking for a revolver, go with a .357. This is a powerful, man-stopping round. The bonus is a .357 revolver will also fire .38 Special rounds, which gives you an option for additional ammunition to seek as need be.

Assault Rifles

Survivalists have a tendency to gravitate toward the "black guns," meaning the civilian versions of various military arms. While the idea of having a semiautomatic submachine gun like an H&K MP5 or an AR-15 has a high "coolness" factor, the reality is that these firearms are expensive and the cost doesn't often balance with the benefits. For the ticket price of a brand new AR-15, you could purchase a good revolver, a great used shotgun, AND two Mosin Nagants.

However, if you've already purchased the other recommended firearms and still have money to burn, there are a few suggestions I'd have for you. The first is the vaunted AK-47. Adding together all the variants, this is believed to be the most popular assault rifle on the planet, with over 100 million of them out there. This popularity is due to both its inexpensive design and its ruggedness. It was designed to be operated by Soviet troops in the dead of winter, so there are no intricate adjustments necessary. It is a bare-bones assault rifle with one purpose: to put holes in something or someone. Shooting the 7.62x39mm cartridge, it has an effective range of a little over 400 yards. With its distinctive curved magazine, the AK-47 is known the world over as a dependable rifle.

The **AR-15** is the civilian version of the U.S. military M16 rifle. It is sometimes referred to as the "Erector Set" of guns because its components can be readily and easily changed. These changes include barrel length as well as any number of aftermarket additions like scopes. Using a 16-inch barrel, a shooter can expect an effective range of around 600 yards or more.

The **Ruger Mini-14** is another great carbine for civilian use. Firing either .223 Remington or 5.56x45mm cartridges, it has an effective range of around 300 yards. While most of the Mini-14s look more sporting than militaristic out of the box, there is a huge assortment of accessories available to create a much tougher appearance, if that is an issue. Back in the 1980s, the Mini-14 gained quite a bit of popularity after being used as the weapon

BUYING USED FIREARMS
by Chance Sanders

Purchasing firearms for your survival arsenal can seem daunting. With new weapons constantly being introduced to the market, it's easy to be persuaded into buying something that you don't need or that is beyond your skill set. For the person who is new to firearms, I suggest looking into the used gun market. Here you'll find firearms of all shapes and sizes in various conditions, and most certainly one or more that suits your needs. Over the years I have purchased many firearms in this manner and have yet to be disappointed.

There are a few concerns you should keep in mind before you buy a firearm. For example, is the firearm a collector's item? If so, expect to pay collector's prices. Understand that firearms companies like to start and stop certain lines of firearms and change things along the way. This can dramatically alter the perceived value of a firearm. Remember, you are trying to put tools in the toolbox, not start a museum.

Another thing to consider is availability of parts for the firearm. On more than one occasion I have had to turn down a great deal on a firearm due to the fact that magazine and other parts were no longer available or extremely hard to find. You are purchasing a weapons system and not just a firearm; consider the cost of care and feeding your system.

Once you have researched and decided what firearms you actually need, it's time to start shopping. One of the best places to find gun deals is in the local classifieds. This allows you to buy from an individual without having to deal with overzealous salesmen, inflated prices, and pesky paperwork. If legal sales between individuals are not prohibited in your state, then this is a preferred method of purchasing weapons.

Beware of deals that seem too good to be true because they usually are. Note that most print classifieds have a corresponding website listing. Items for sale are often up on the website days before they appear in print. This is important to keep in mind because the good deals go fast.

Another great place to purchase used firearms is at a gun store. This is a method that I have had great success with, however it does require a keen eye and cash money in your pocket. I tend to make frequent trips in and out of the gun stores that I visit. I will often just sit in the parking lot and wait. What I am doing is watching the other patrons of the store go in and out. If I see someone going in with a gun case and coming out a short time later with the same case, then I can determine that the individual was seeking to sell his or her firearm, but no agreement could be reached. I simply introduce myself and ask politely about the firearm. This has led to some of the best deals I have ever received.

A drawback of purchasing a used gun is that you have little or no guarantee as to whether the gun will function once you get it home. If you buy from a reputable dealer, you may be able to get your money back. If you are concerned about this when buying from an individual, meet up at the local gun range to test the weapon before making your purchase.

Please take these things into consideration before spending your hard-earned money. A well-thought-out arsenal will not only bring you satisfaction now, but will be there in the future should you need it.

Chance Sanders served eight years as a Marine Corps infantryman and has written numerous articles on weapons and survival. Chance is also the public face of Mission Knives and owner of Last Chance Productions.

of choice for members of the A-Team on the TV show of that name.

Here's the thing about assault rifles. There is certainly something to be said for having the ability to send thirty or so rounds out with reasonable accuracy in about thirty seconds. That is a lot of firepower made available to the shooter. But, assault rifles are expensive, both to own and to feed. If your budget allows, by all means have at it. But only if you've already taken care of the basics as outlined earlier.

Purchasing Firearms and Accessories

In the following sections we'll discuss a few factors that you should keep in mind when shopping for firearms and accessories.

AMMUNITION

How much ammunition should you stockpile? The cheeky answer is, you can never store too much. But obviously there should be some sort of goal to achieve. I would recommend at least ten thousand rounds of .22 ammunition, for starters. At $2 for a box of fifty, this equates to roughly $400. That's a hefty chunk of change to lay out in one purchase, so spread it out. Every time you visit the store, pick up one or two boxes. It will add up quickly, trust me.

For your shotgun, the ideal would be to have at least a hundred shells on hand. That's going to be a hefty hit on the wallet. Buy a little at a time and build up your supply as you can.

For your distance shooter, aim for five hundred to a thousand rounds. Remember, this and your .22 are going to be the firearms that not only provide protection and defense but hopefully put meat on the table.

Ammunition for handguns can get pricey in a hurry. The good news is handgun ammunition is usually sold in boxes of 50 or 100 so you won't have to purchase many boxes to reach a goal of around 750 rounds or so.

ACCESSORIES

For each firearm, you will want a full cleaning kit and as well as spare parts. I would highly recommend you ask your local firearms dealer about having someone teach you how to field-strip, fully clean and oil, and reassemble every firearm you purchase. Go through the cleaning process each and every single time you are done firing the weapon. Also get into the habit of routinely cleaning your firearms any time they have sat for a while without being used. If you treat your guns properly, they will last generations.

Experiment with different slings and holsters to find ones that are comfortable for you. Remember, in a world without law, you're going to want to have your firearms on you or within very close reach at all times. You may find, for example, that a pancake holster at the small of your back is much more comfortable than one that rides on your hip.

For your long guns, invest in good-quality scopes. Be sure whatever scopes you decide to purchase will indeed work well with the weapons you'll be using. Some brand names to look for are Tasco, Leupold, and Trijicon.

RELOADING EQUIPMENT

Many survivalists own and regularly use reloading equipment. This is not at all a bad idea. Having the ability to reload your own cartridges will greatly extend your ammunition stores, as long as you have stockpiled the requisite components. However, for those just starting out acquiring firearms and becoming comfortable with their use, I'd much rather you concentrate on stocking up on commercially produced ammunition than overloading your plate, so to speak. Being able to reload isn't going to do you much good if you can't hit your target because you lack practice. But yes, definitely consider reloading supplies and skills for later acquisition.

CHAPTER 8
Other Weapons

While firearms and other things that go boom will likely be your primary weapons, they should by no means be your only ones. There are many different scenarios where you may need a weapon that is either silent or is easy to have with you at all times. Before we get into the sorts of weapons you should consider having on hand and practicing with, let's talk a bit about the weapons to disregard.

Ineffective Weapons

Throwing stars, known by their proper name as shuriken, are, for all practical purposes, worthless to the survivalist. First, despite what Hollywood would have you think, they were never intended to be used to kill. They were only used as distractions and a means to discourage pursuit. Second, it takes an awful lot of practice to be able to hit even a stationary target more than about 10 feet away, let alone a living target who is moving around. I'd agree that they are fun to play around with but you shouldn't consider them to be a viable weapon.

Throwing knives are also a bad idea. Again, it takes quite a bit of time tossing knives at foam and wooden targets before you'll become even close to proficient. Second, even a very skilled knife thrower has few options for any sort of kill shot on a human. If the target is wearing a heavy coat, the blade of the knife likely won't penetrate much beyond the skin. And forget all about headshots; that's more silver screen nonsense. Another thing to think about is this: Let's say you got lucky enough to actually hit your attacker with a throwing knife. If it doesn't kill him, what would stop him from pulling the knife from his arm or leg and, well, returning it to you?

Another item of dubious value to the survivalist, at least as far as an offensive weapon, is the blowgun. While it may have some use for small game hunting, it is all but worthless against people. Sure, a very skilled (or lucky) marksman might be able to hit an eyeball from 10 feet out or so. But honestly, you'd probably do better using the blowgun to jab at the attacker's face and skip the darts altogether.

Unless you are seriously trained in their use, avoid swords. Personally, if given the choice, I'd rather go empty-handed against someone holding a sword over someone holding a knife. Unless you really know what you're doing, swords can be very awkward and difficult to control effectively. Amateurs tend to swing them like baseball bats, which is easy to predict and counter.

With those out of the way, let's move on to some weapons that will have value for the survivalist.

Fighting Knives

As ought to be fairly obvious, this category includes all manner of sharp, pointy objects. At the core, fighting with a knife will involve trying to inflict two types of injuries on your opponent. A cutting slash will cause pain and blood loss, but rarely if ever will it take the person down quickly. That will require penetration, preferably to a vital organ, which is the second type of injury.

Bear in mind that even highly trained elite soldiers will avoid fighting with blades if humanly possible. Let's face it, blades can be scary and the thought of being cut by one in a fight is enough to set anyone's nerves on edge. If there is one absolute truth about knife fighting, it is that whether you win or lose, you will get cut, probably more than once.

I am not discounting the value of having a knife on your hip as a last-ditch weapon. What I am saying, though, is that if you find yourself in a situation where you need to rely on that blade to save your life, you screwed up somewhere along the way. You've either run out of ammunition for your firearm or lost it somehow, and you've allowed your attacker to get close enough that your only option is to pull your blade and hope for the best. This is not anywhere close to an ideal situation. When I say the knife is your last-ditch weapon, I mean exactly that. You should have exhausted every other possible option, including retreat, before resorting to fighting with a blade.

However, the prudent survivalist prepares for every conceivable eventuality, and knife fighting is one of those

PLAIN OR SERRATED KNIVES?

With some models of fighting knives, you have an option of plain, serrated, or partially serrated. While I'll allow that serrations allow for ease in cutting rope and other materials, particularly when those materials are wet, I generally avoid serrations on my blades. The serrated edges can be difficult, if not impossible, to sharpen in the field without specialized equipment.

possibilities. A knife fight is not the place for anything flashy or elaborate. You want and need to put the other person down as quickly as possible. As you consider the myriad different types of knives with which you might arm yourself, bear in mind that different blade styles are suited for different applications. Here are a few blade styles that are well suited for fighting:

CLIP POINT BLADE   The clip point blade is where the forward part of the blade looks like a part has been cut or clipped out, usually on a curve. This part of the blade is called the false edge and may or may not be sharpened. Even if it is not sharpened, this false edge is thinner than the spine of the blade. This serves to create a very sharp point on the blade and thus it is very suitable for thrusting attacks causing deep penetration. The blades are usually wide and thick, which gives them the strength to withstand abuse. The famous Ka-Bar knife of the U.S. Marines has a clip point blade, as does the well-known Bowie knife.

FAIRBAIRN-SYKES KNIFE   The Fairbairn-Sykes knife is an example of a stiletto-style blade. It is double-edged and comes to a very sharp point. It was designed by William Fairbairn and Eric Sykes after both had spent time serving on the Shanghai Municipal Police before World War II. The knife became well known after being issued to the Special Air Service (SAS) and British Commandos. This style of blade is designed primarily for thrusting attacks with the double edges allowing for quick and deep penetration.

TANTO BLADES   Tanto blades are sharp angles rather than curves, with a chisel point that permits fast, deep penetration. A well-made tanto blade will be able to go through a car door with no damage to the tip of the knife. The Cold Steel company (www.ColdSteel.com) made a name for itself back in the 1980s when it began producing high-quality and very strong tanto blades. It has since become a leader in the production of fairly high-end blades at affordable prices.

KUKRI KNIFE   The kukri knife is usually fairly large, landing somewhere between an average belt knife and a machete. You'll notice the odd shape of the blade—thinner near the handle and wider toward the tip—as well as the angle of the blade. The kukri knife was specifically designed to decapitate foes as well as handle other heavy-duty chopping chores. This makes it a potentially devastating weapon, but difficult to handle without practice. It should go without saying that the kukri isn't designed for thrusting attacks but for sweeping swings.

BLADE LENGTH

Although a shorter blade has its drawbacks, as we discussed about folding knives, it isn't completely worthless. You just have to bear in mind its limitations. You can't expect a 3-inch blade to be effective when targeting a lung, but it will work great on the carotid artery or an eye. A push knife is one example of a good short-bladed fighting knife. With these knives, the blade protrudes from the middle of the handle, fitting between your fingers as you close your fist around it. Most of these types of knives have blades just a few inches long but they can be lethal in even an untrained hand.

A fighting knife should have a blade of at least 5 or 6 inches. This gives you enough length to penetrate outerwear and clothing and reach vital organs. However, too long of a blade can be cumbersome and awkward for many people.

CONSTRUCTION AND MATERIALS

In addition to blade length, another consideration when selecting a fighting knife is how it is constructed. You want something that has a full tang. What this means is that the blade actually runs completely through the handle of the knife, rather than being a separate unit that is affixed to a handle. A full tang allows for much greater strength and durability.

Many of the "survival knives" marketed in the last couple decades are cheaply made and will probably break under even the slightest abuse. Hollow-handle knives were hugely popular back in the 1980s and 1990s due to

FOLDING KNIVES

I highly advise you to not consider any type of folding knife as anything more than a tool. While it is possible to draw and open a folding knife quickly, the blades are generally nowhere near long enough to inflict serious damage to an opponent.

For a fighting knife, you are going to need a blade at least 5 or 6 inches long. Much shorter than that and you'll have difficulty reaching anything vital when you thrust. Bear in mind, most people today have at least a bit of belly fat. Add to that a jacket or coat and you're talking at least a few inches of, well, padding, before you get to vital organs. Could you dispatch someone with a smaller folding knife? Sure you could. I could cut through a 2x4 with a hacksaw too, given enough time and effort. But use the proper tool for the job whenever possible.

being featured in the first couple Rambo movies starring Sylvester Stallone. While they are not quite as popular anymore, you'll still see them at flea markets and such. While a select few models are well made, most of the ones you'll find are very cheaply manufactured and the blades will break off the handle easily.

The blade should be fairly thick along the spine, somewhere in the neighborhood of ⅜-inch or so. Thinner blades are more likely to bend or even snap under pressure.

Another thing to consider is the type of metal used for the blade. Look for a good quality steel alloy, like 440C. Avoid any blades that are marked as coming from China or Pakistan. Another good option that holds an edge well is 1095. ATS-34 is a Japanese stainless steel and is superior to 440C in terms of keeping an edge, but it is not as rust-resistant. Carbon is the hardening element added to steel blades and makes for a tougher metal. Thus, look for blades that are marketed as "high carbon."

For handle material, consider both durability and texture. There is a wide range of materials available, from wood to plastic. Remember, you may be fighting with wet hands, especially if they are soaked with blood, so you want a handle that won't slip from your grasp. A good, deep checkered texture will do well.

Some knives come with paracord-wrapped handles, which isn't an inherently bad idea. Any good prepper knows the value of having as much paracord with them as possible, given how incredibly useful it is.

The handle is also the primary component of the comfort of the knife. A knife really isn't something I'd suggest buying online, sight unseen. You should hold it in your hand first, checking out the balance as well as the comfort. With that said though, there is nothing wrong with visiting a few stores in person, deciding on the knife you like best, then shopping around online for the best price.

One of the best knives I've owned is my Becker Combat Bowie. The blade is thick and strong while retaining a razor edge. It is heavy but comfortable in my hand. While Becker knives are on the pricey side, you truly get what you pay for.

GUARDS, POMMELS, AND SHEATHS

I personally like a good guard on a fighting knife. This prevents your fingers from slipping from the handle onto the blade. Another feature on many fighting knives is a hole in the handle where you can attach a lanyard. Should you decide to affix a lanyard to your knife, I'd advise you to not loop it around your wrist when engaging in battle. What can happen is, when you thrust your knife into your target, the target's body will naturally pull away. If your knife is caught in the target—by their clothing, a rib, whatever—and you have the lanyard looped around your wrist, you could be pulled off balance.

Many fighting knives today also have a reinforced pommel that can be used to strike your opponent. While I'm all about having options in a fight, personally I figure if you're close enough to bop them on the skull with the pommel of your knife, you're close enough to do more damage with the blade.

For the sheath, you want something that will sit comfortably on your belt, preferably with various carrying position options. The sheath should be well constructed and sturdy. You don't want a cheap nylon sheath but rather something either leather or good plastic like Kydex. Multiple carrying positions give you options depending on the situation. Working out in the field pulling weeds, you may be fine with it hanging off your belt to your hip. When patrolling, you may prefer it to be on a chest rig or attached horizontally at the small of your back. This is primarily a personal decision, of course, based on individual preference. Personally, I don't care for having a knife bouncing against my hip when I run and while I could tie the end of the sheath to my thigh, I find that uncomfortable as well. But, to each his or her own.

Martial Arts Weapons

On a regular basis, I see or hear people mentioning their intention to use various martial arts weapons for post-collapse defense. These include:

BO   A staff, usually of wood, anywhere from 3 to 6 feet in length.

NUNCHUKU   Frequently erroneously called "nun-chucks," two dowels connected by a length of cord or chain.

KAMA   A short length of dowel with a sickle-shaped blade on the end. Traditionally these are used in pairs.

TONFA   A short baton with a handle extending from the side. The PR-24 police baton is modeled after the tonfa.

Unless you are extensively trained in the use of these or other martial arts weapons, consider them to be nothing more than novelty items at best. Don't get me wrong, in trained hands any of these martial arts weapons can be devastatingly lethal. In untrained hands though... perhaps not so much. While it is true that any weapon is better than none, at least in most scenarios, with many martial arts weapons you can just as easily injure yourself as you could an opponent. Swinging a pair of nunchuku around your head, trying to nail the other guy, you just might clobber yourself. At that point, your best hope is your opponent critically injures himself while he's rolling on the floor laughing.

Should you decide you just have to have martial arts weapons in your arsenal, I would encourage you to shop around for both price and quality. The katana you see advertised for $19.95 will probably snap in half the first time you hit anything harder than an orange, let alone a human body. If you go the cheap route, don't fantasize about going all Super Samurai on a group of MZBs. Try that and you'll be back to hoping for laughter-induced cardiac arrest to come to your rescue.

Pepper Spray

The idea behind the use of pepper spray is to incapacitate your attacker long enough for you to take action, whether it be fleeing or using lethal force against them. In and of itself, pepper spray is generally not fatal. The range can be somewhat limited and, depending upon the delivery method, that range can be greatly affected by wind.

Bear in mind too that you can substitute products like wasp/hornet spray and bear repellent for actual OC spray. But, doing so does expose one to lawsuits and possibly criminal prosecution, so that should be reserved for a time when the laws no longer apply.

Electroshock Weapons

These include stun guns in all their many varieties, as well as Taser-type weapons. These all work on the same principle: delivering a high-voltage shock to the aggres-

SELECTING THE RIGHT PEPPER SPRAY
by Steve Thibeault

Unless you're facing off with someone holding a gun, pepper spray is a very effective product for self-defense; it's immediate, painful, and completely changes the priorities of your attacker. Be sure to get a spray that is actual "pepper" spray made from peppers; the main ingredient for these is oleoresin capsicum (OC). Other sprays such as tear gas are irritants and take several seconds to have an effect. Real pepper spray is an inflammatory agent, not an irritant. It inflames the mucous membranes and capillaries, forces the eyes to slam shut, and severely restricts normal breathing. The effect is intense pain that can last for up to forty-five minutes.

Pepper sprays come in many sizes, from a small key chain spray on up to a 1-pound canister used for crowd dispersal. These smaller sizes can be kept on your belt or placed into a purse. Or stash them around the house at entryways so you will always have one available if someone comes to the door.

If you need to do any traveling on foot or otherwise, a larger canister may be what you want. If you have multiple assailants, a bigger can will be enough to incapacitate them.

Pepper spray comes in many formulations usually specified by a percentage. A minimum of 10% is what you want to look for (higher percentages are available but they all are similarly effective). A popular, effective brand is the Wildfire 18% Pepper Spray. Its formulation is made in the same factory as other police sprays but is designed for civilian use. Police want to subdue their suspect, but for the effect to wear off quickly so they can process them. As a civilian, you don't care how long the spray's effects last. In fact, the longer it takes, the more time you have to get away.

Another factor to consider is the way the spray comes out of the canister. The two main methods are stream and fogger. A stream fires straight, is more controllable, and is less affected by wind. A fogger has a wider dispersal pattern and is good for calm or windless conditions (such as indoors) or when your aim is not going to be that great.

Gel sprays are slightly more expensive but spraying a sticky gelatinous substance into someone's face is not something they can get rid of easily. The more they rub it away, the more deeply it will ingrain itself into the skin. Gel is also not affected as much by wind and you can aim it well.

Bear spray is also a pepper spray. This is specially formulated for bears and shoots out in a shotgun-blast-dispersal pattern. If a bear charges, spray toward the bear, creating a virtual wall that the bear has to run through. Once the bear hits this wall, it will have to stop in order to contend with not being able to see or breathe very well.

At the very least, consider pepper spray as a non-lethal and very effective self-defense product. It can be used from a distance, which serves to keep the attacker or assailant away from you. Unlike CS or tear gas, which people can develop a tolerance to, pepper spray affects even those on drugs or alcohol. It is also one of the most inexpensive forms of personal protection available on any budget.

After serving in the army for eleven years, Steve Thibeault began helping people learn to protect themselves with non-lethal self-defense products. His website, www.TBOtech.com, has become the premier destination for finding personal and home protection items on the Internet. As an avid outdoorsman, his interest in survival guided him to also develop www.Survival-Gear.com with the goal of providing top-quality survival kits people can actually depend on.

sor. This causes the muscles to spasm, which results in pain and incapacitation. The difference between stun guns and Tasers is that the stun guns require the user to make contact with the aggressor with the business end of the stun gun, whereas the Taser type of weapon shoots projectiles that are connected to the base unit through wires. The projectiles, typically small barbed needles, make contact with the aggressor and the high-voltage discharge is transmitted through the wires.

How effective are they? I recently watched a video that was taken during a training session at a local police department. The officers were being trained in the use of a Taser and as part of their training, each was subjected to having the needles from a unit taped to the calf of their leg. Once affixed, the unit was activated for about three or four seconds. I know most of these officers personally and they are big guys, strong and in great condition. Every single one of them screamed like a little girl when that voltage hit them.

Stun guns, as noted earlier, require the user to actually make contact with the aggressor with the unit. Doing so while the unit is activated sends the voltage from one electrode on the unit into the attacker and back out to the other electrode. These stun guns come in a wide range of styles, from small ones that look like lipstick tubes to large batons. With the variations in size come similar differences in the voltage used.

Either type of electroshock weapon will allow you to stop an attacker in their tracks, often putting them completely on the ground long enough for you to take further action.

Improvised Weapons

Generally speaking, most improvised weapons will either be a blunt melee weapon or some variation on a knife or dagger. Baseball bats, with or without nails driven into them, are an example of a blunt melee weapon. A short piece of rebar filed to a point on one end would be an example of a dagger.

This photo is of an improvised spike I made a few years ago. I came across this tool used for removing locking hubcaps on a car I owned. It was just a matter of a few minutes on a grinding wheel to turn the slotted screwdriver end into a very sharp spike. I could go a step further and wrap the handle in friction tape to finish off the weapon. Holding the handle with the spike protruding from between the fingers in a closed fist makes for a very deadly weapon.

There is no limit to the ingenuity and creativity of a human being bent on the destruction of another. Prisons are chock-full of examples of this, with weapons made from everything from toothbrushes to rolled up newspapers and magazines.

A fairly common improvised weapon many are familiar with is lighting the output of a can of hairspray, making sort of an improvised flamethrower. While impressive and certainly effective in some situations, you'd have to consider the possibility that the person you just lit on fire isn't going to lie down nicely right away but is likely to go rampaging through the home or retreat. This may cause you some problems, such as fire spreading until you can put that attacker down.

Another idea I've seen brought up a time or two is to take breakable containers of bleach and ammonia, tape them together, then throw them into a crowd of attackers. The idea here is that the two chemicals will combine on impact and the resulting toxic cloud will harm the attackers. However, if this were to be done in an open area, such as a backyard, the effect would be minimal to anyone who doesn't happen to be standing right next to the impact. Trying this in an enclosed area, such as the home or retreat, will probably have just as much negative impact on the residents as on the attackers.

Molotov cocktails could prove useful against attackers in the backyard. For the few who may not be familiar with them, you simply fill a glass bottle with a flammable liquid such as gasoline and stopper the end with a long piece of cloth. Time permitting, you could even use duct tape to make sure the cloth stays put. Just before using, tip the bottle over and let some of the liquid soak into the cloth. You then light the cloth and throw the bottle. When it lands, it shatters and the flaming cloth sets the liquid ablaze. It is very effective and, to be honest, rather impressive-looking when it hits the ground. You can increase the effectiveness by adding soap flakes to the liquid. This thickens the liquid and helps it stick to whatever it lands on, whether that is a vehicle or a few people bent on your demise.

When considering all the different types of defensive weapons available to the survivalist, remember that the best weapon on the planet resides between your ears. Use common sense, logic, and your ability to think on your feet to make the necessary decisions rapidly yet effectively.

CHAPTER 9

Hand-to-Hand Combat

If a conflict comes to the point where you have to resort to empty-hand combat, you have failed in your defensive measures at some point. Make no mistake about it, going toe to toe with an attacker is an absolute last resort. Often, it would be a better course of action to retreat and make your stand another day. But in the event that option is not available, you'll need to plan accordingly. In this chapter we'll look at some of the ways you might be able to defend yourself without a weapon.

Martial Arts

While many martial arts started out as absolutely devastating ways to disarm and incapacitate an opponent, most of them have been watered down over the years. While there may be very practical self-defense techniques still taught, the focus is usually on just creating an opening whereby you can disengage from the conflict and get away.

Don't get me wrong, that's a great idea in today's society. But in a post-collapse world where calling 911 isn't an option, you need to learn how to take your opponent down and keep him there, perhaps permanently. Doing otherwise will just mean he will be coming at you again, perhaps better prepared and better armed.

One advantage of taking classes in a martial art is that you will learn not only how to throw a punch, but also how to take one. You will learn the proper way to fall to avoid injury and you'll learn how much it hurts when someone hits and kicks you. This is a good thing, as many people have never truly been in a fight before and have little understanding of how pain and adrenaline will affect them.

Fights in the real world are rarely ever like they are presented on the silver screen. Teeth are lost, ribs are bruised and broken, knuckles get cut up. There is a good reason why fistfights are referred to as "swapping skin" in some parts of the country. But at least some of the risk can be mitigated by learning how to fight effectively and efficiently.

There are a few martial arts taught today that I feel have particular value to the survivalist. Check around your local area to see if such training is available to you. Be sure to do your homework with regard to the instructors and do everything you can to make sure they are appropriately licensed or otherwise authorized to teach the art. Most reputable schools or dojos will allow prospective students to sit in a class or two and observe how the classes are run.

KRAV MAGA

Israeli Defense Force Chief Instructor Imi Sde-Or developed this brutally effective martial art in the 1940s and 1950s. He had a wealth of experience in both wrestling and boxing and eventually sought to create a defensive art that would combine that knowledge with the more practical aspects of street fighting. Today, Krav Maga is taught to police agencies and military forces around the world.

One of the most important aspects of Krav Maga, and one that is particularly of interest to preppers, is that it seeks to finish a fight as quickly as possible. Striking vulnerable areas of the body is a main focus. There are no elaborate and showy forms to learn. Instead, Krav Maga is all about winning the fight as quickly and decisively as possible. This is not a martial art well suited for competitions and tournaments.

Various types of hand strikes and kicks are taught, though contrary to what most people think when the term "martial arts" comes up, the kicks are generally low and aimed at vulnerable points such as the knee, rather than the high-flying spin kicks often seen on late night TV. Furthermore, despite the art's focus on staying off the ground with your opponent, it does include several techniques that involve fighting from the ground.

In addition to attack strategies, students learn how to defend against a wide range of weapons, from bats to firearms. Many of the defensive actions taught incorporate a counterattack. The idea is to turn the conflict from defense to attack quickly. Situational awareness is also taught so students become more adept at recognizing potential threats and can quickly take appropriate action.

Students train at "full speed," meaning the attacks and defenses are practiced in the same way they would be applied in the real world rather than at half-strength, as is the case in many other martial arts. Naturally, safety precautions are taken to prevent injury. The techniques are taught and practiced in many different conditions, such as in low light to simulate night conflicts and in confined spaces like alleyways.

ESKRIMA/KALI

The term "Eskrima" refers to the traditional weapon-based martial arts of the Philippines. Known as Kali in the United States, this art focuses on the use of sticks, blades, and improvised weapons. As is the case with many traditional martial arts, it arose out of the need for common people to defend themselves from attacking forces.

Unlike many other arts, in Eskrima students are taught how to use weapons first and fight empty-handed later. Part of the reason for this is that many of the movements and techniques taught with the weapons are virtually identical to the movements used without weapons. Thus, muscle memory is already present when the student advances to empty-hand techniques. Students learn various strikes as well as defensive blocks and joint locks.

Another unique feature of Eskrima is that students are taught to use two weapons at the same time, one in each hand. Gradually, the student learns to be ambidextrous when fighting. This also comes into play when the student

PANANJAKMAN

Pananjakman is an integral part of traditional Eskrima, despite sometimes being marketed separately in the United States. It refers to striking techniques using and directed to the legs and feet. The goal is usually to incapacitate the opponent by forcing joints like knees and ankles to bend in painful directions, often causing dislocation or fractures.

begins learning empty-hand techniques. If a practitioner has only one weapon, the empty hand is called the live hand. Where in many other fighting styles the empty hand would be hidden or protected in some way to prevent injury, in Eskrima it is used to trap the opponent's weapon or apply joint-lock techniques.

The weapons typically used in Eskrima are sticks and knives. The concentration on such weapons is of particular interest to the survivalist, as those are two items that can often be easily scrounged up if need be. The sticks range in length from 4 inches to a few feet, and as noted earlier, are often paired.

Various bladed weapons are also used, such as the bolo, which is a type of machete, and the balisong knife, commonly referred to in the United States as a butterfly knife. Other bladed weapons include the karambit (seen to the right), the balang, and the kris knife, noted for its wavy blade. Many of the weapon-based techniques translate easily to improvised weapons like ice picks, flashlights, and bottles.

NINJUTSU

First, forget everything you've seen on TV and in the movies. The fictional ninja has very little to do with the real art of Ninjutsu. For example, in ancient Japan, the ubiquitous *shuriken* (throwing stars) weren't routinely buried into the foreheads of enemies from a football field away. Instead, they were used as distractions, giving the ninja time to escape.

Ninjutsu began in the mountainous areas of Japan in the 7th century. While the samurai of the day had the best of everything in terms of equipment and weapons, the ninja had to make do with what they could make themselves. Therefore, the samurai had beautiful and highly prized swords while the ninja had shorter bladed weapons that were created with more concern for functionality than appearance. The ninja, more so than practitioners of most other martial arts, became experts in subterfuge and also in the use of ingenious gadgets and equipment to aid their efforts.

The Japanese symbol for ninja actually directly translates to endurance, tolerance, or strength. Students learn not only armed and unarmed combat techniques but concealment, military strategy, explosives, herbal healing, and even meteorology. Their hand-to-hand combat training is very much based in reality and includes techniques designed to quickly incapacitate an opponent, whether they are armed or not.

REAL NINJUTSU
by Jon F. Merz

My friend and fellow author Jon F. Merz has studied Ninjutsu for much of his life. I asked him for his opinion on how practical Ninjutsu would be for preppers. Here's what he had to say.

As a student of authentic Ninjutsu for over twenty years, I can tell you that the art is extremely well suited to preppers. Ninjutsu is based on natural body movement and emphasizes practicality over flashy movements. Anyone can do it. You don't need to be in Olympian shape and the moves rely on simple actions that produce devastating results. Think minimum effort, maximum results. Developed as it was on the battlefields and during covert action in feudal Japan, Ninjutsu remains as applicable today as it was when Japan was embroiled in civil war.

Ninjutsu encompasses every aspect of combat, from unarmed striking, grappling, joint locks, and throws to improvised and unorthodox weapons, weapons retention skills, up to and including strategic application and mind sciences. As legendary as the myth of Ninjutsu invisibility is, it is based on pragmatic practices that work on many levels.

Traditional Ninja used "traveling disguises" when on missions that enabled them to blend in with their

While it may be difficult to find a reputable Ninjutsu instructor in your area, given that this art has attracted more "wannabes" than perhaps any other martial art, if you find a good local class, I'd encourage you to consider attending.

environments. Disguised as entertainers, monks, merchants, fortune tellers, and masterless samurai, they were able to ensure that they did not stand out in a hostile territory. Modern Ninjutsu practitioners employ similar concepts to reduce their own "friction" within an environment. Do you know how to order wine and sample it? Do you speak a smattering of other languages? Even a simple greeting can help ensure you blend in. Modern ninja try to develop themselves to the point where they can seamlessly move through everyday life without causing any friction; this means knowing how to act and appear in such a way that you never stand out unless you want to. The highest level of this development is to become the "gray man," the person you see on the street or in a hotel or anywhere…and then five seconds later, you can't remember them.

The practicality of Ninjutsu, combined with its higher teachings, makes it a fantastic method of self-protection for anyone interested in preparing for what might be coming.

Jon F. Merz has trained with Mark Davis, Chief Instructor of the Boston Martial Arts Center (www.BostonMartialArts.com) in Boston, Massachusetts, for over twenty years and is a fifth-degree black belt in the art. Jon's personal website is www.JonFMerz.net.

FIGHTING DIRTY

Assuming you have had little or no actual combat training in real world self-defense techniques, let's talk about the differences between Hollywood, competition-style martial arts and reality. First, if you are fighting for your life, remember: There are no rules. In tournaments, it is usually against the rules to go for your opponent's groin. In the real world, the groin is a primary target. Pulling hair, twisting and breaking fingers, and gouging eyes are all fair game. (With all the diseases running rampant today and likely to be worse down the road, I'd avoid biting, though.) The objective is to win at all costs.

Second, spend any time watching the latest action hero onscreen and you'll believe that high-flying kicks and flipping over your opponent are great ways to engage in battle. It should go without saying that those techniques have little to no application in the real world. Jump into the air to spin a kick at your opponent's head and you're likely to end up flat on your back with his boot on your throat. Save the acrobatics for tournaments.

Many effective techniques would probably be considered fighting "dirty" in certain contexts. When it comes to an actual life-or-death confrontation, there is no dirty fighting, only fighting to win.

USE YOUR NATURAL WEAPONS

While you may be unarmed when it comes to conventional or even improvised weapons, you have many natural tools available to you for defense. First, use your head. I mean that in both senses of the term. Use your brain to think on your feet and don't let panic overtake you. Being able to remain calm while thinking on your feet will do more for you in a fight than learning any ten dirty tricks. Quite often, the winner in a fight isn't necessarily the strongest nor the quickest. The victor is usually the one who is willing to do whatever it takes to succeed.

In terms of the physical body weapons at your disposal, your skull, especially the forehead area, is extremely hard. A head butt to your opponent's nose will likely not only be unexpected but will definitely cause quite a bit of pain. Trust me, the adrenaline flowing through your body will deaden any pain you might experience from this technique.

Let's look at the rest of the natural weapons you have at your disposal:

ELBOWS   The point of the elbow is almost impossible to fracture and will serve you well when applied to the kidneys, ribs, and other targets. Unless you've trained in the technique, avoid sweeping the elbow up and across your opponent. Instead, use it like a chisel to hammer down into your target.

HANDS   Obviously your hands are valuable self-defense weapons. A clenched fist is very hard and works well when applied with great force to many body targets. Avoid striking bony areas, such as the ribs, unless you've been trained in how to do so properly; otherwise you risk fracturing your own hand. The webbing that runs from your index finger to your thumb is an often-overlooked tool. Use it to strike your opponent's throat to damage their trachea. Use your fingers for poking eyes, grabbing ears or hair, and twisting limbs.

KNEES   Knees are used somewhat like elbows. A solid knee to the groin works better than many other flashier techniques. If your opponent is on the ground, dropping knee-first into the kidneys or solar plexus will probably end the confrontation.

FEET   Never try to kick your opponent with your bare feet. Doing so only invites a broken toe or other damage. However, a solid kick with a hiking boot to the opponent's knee will work wonders in changing their attitude. Never kick above the waist unless your opponent is on the ground; it is all too easy for them to grab your flailing foot and twist you to the ground.

POTENTIAL TARGETS

When engaging in hand-to-hand combat, there are many different body targets to bear in mind. Keep your wits about you and exploit any openings you are given. Let's go over the potential targets, from head to toe.

TEMPLE   A solid blow to the side of the head can render your opponent unconscious. If the blow is hard enough, it can kill.

HAIR   Not only does pulling hair cause pain, it can serve as a handhold to move your opponent in the direction you wish.

EYES   If your opponent cannot see you, it makes his job vastly more difficult. Using a thumbnail, you can scratch the eyeball or even gouge the entire eyeball out of the socket. Even a strike coming near the eyes will cause your opponent to flinch away, distracting him and allowing you to follow up with another technique.

NOSE   Landing a blow to the nose will first cause the eyes to water, which obscures vision. And of course a broken nose will bleed quite a bit, which will serve to impair their breathing, in addition to being very painful.

EARS   A slap on the ear(s) can cause the eardrums to rupture. Not only will this affect hearing, but it can also cause dizziness and disorientation. Grabbing an ear and tearing it from the head will obviously cause great pain.

MOUTH Despite Hollywood conventions to the contrary, I generally instruct people to avoid aiming strikes at the mouth. The main reason is that doing so will possibly risk getting their saliva into an open cut on your hand, potentially infecting you with disease. With that said though, knocking out a tooth or three will cause extreme pain.

NECK A strike across the front of the throat can crush the trachea, causing suffocation. The carotid arteries, the main blood vessels supplying blood to the brain, run from top to bottom on each side of the neck. Interrupting this blood flow for several seconds will render the opponent unconscious. Twisting the head savagely at the neck can also kill instantly.

SOLAR PLEXUS A solid hit to the area in the middle of the chest, just below the sternum, can cause the diaphragm to spasm. This can cause your opponent to have difficulty breathing.

RIBS While an untrained fighter may find these difficult to break, doing so may drive a fractured rib into a lung.

KIDNEYS Striking these can cause extreme pain. Aim for the lower back, to either side of the spine, and use either a closed fist or an elbow.

FINGERS These can be broken fairly easily if twisted or bent violently.

GROIN This is an obvious target. Even glancing blows can be very painful and render your opponent "down for the count." While the tendency is to use knees to strike this area, don't overlook a technique called "monkey grabbing the peach." Grab, twist, pull.

KNEES   It takes very little pressure to dislocate a knee, making it very difficult for your opponent to stand. Aim a kick to the side of the knee. Glancing the kick across the front of the knee will move the kneecap out of position, where a solid blow to the side of the joint will cause dislocation.

FEET/TOES   A stomp on the top of the foot can fracture the delicate bones and/or break a toe or two.

Remember, in any combat situation, armed or unarmed, there are no rules. There is no such thing as a "fair fight." There is a winner and there is a loser, simple as that. Do everything in your power to make sure you are on the winning side of the equation.

SECTION IV

OTHER CONSIDERATIONS

CHAPTER 10
Guard Dogs

Let me say up front that I've always been a "dog person." I love dogs and have owned them all my life. I find they are loyal friends who stick by you through thick and thin. I couldn't imagine going through any sort of stressful time in my life without having a canine companion by my side. Some folks think of their dogs as employees or even just cattle. For me, dogs are family and are treated as such.

Guard Dog versus Watch Dog

People often use "guard dog" and "watch dog" interchangeably. The reality is, that is sort of like putting security guards and S.W.A.T. members in the same group. The essential functions do relate to one another but they are worlds apart in practice.

Before we get into the differences between those two roles, let's first discuss the desirable traits common to both.

INTELLIGENCE A high level of intelligence is critical. While dogs

DOG BREEDERS

If you are considering investing in a purebred dog, whether for security or just as a family pet, it pays to do your homework. There are many, many disreputable breeders out there. Whenever possible, ask for direct referrals from family, friends, and coworkers. When you visit the breeder, you want to see not only the animals available for purchase but also their parents. Observe the adult dogs to get a good indicator of what the puppies will grow to resemble, not just in size and color but also in temperament.

However, don't overlook your local animal shelter as a source for a watchdog. First, you may be surprised at how many purebred dogs end up in shelters, either as runaways or as owner surrenders. Second, mutts should never be discounted as potential security animals. Mixed breeds often suffer fewer health problems, particularly age-related issues like hip dysplasia. Quite often, mutts are the perfect combination of desirable traits from their mixed lineage with few if any of the negative qualities.

are like people in that intelligence varies with the individual, some breeds (such as the German shepherd) are known for possessing a high degree of innate intelligence. Trainability is part of the overall intelligence of the dog.

TEMPERAMENT   Temperament refers to how the dog reacts, mentally and physically, to the world around it. A dog who is perpetually scared of a leaf blowing by in the wind will naturally not be the greatest choice as an addition to your security plan. The dog's level of aggressiveness, or perhaps a better term is assertiveness, is part of its temperament as well. Being bold and not backing down from what it feels is the right action are welcome traits in a security dog. Naturally, a dog who is overly aggressive is not what you want. You want a dog who will act, or can be trained to act, in an appropriate manner.

LOYALTY   Loyalty is also extremely important. The ideal dog will easily bond to you and your family, seeing itself as part of your "pack." This bond is what compels the dog to protect you.

WATCH DOGS

Watch dogs are part of your Early Warning System. Their job is to alert you to potential danger, primarily through barking. Watch dogs need not be large or strong. They won't be physically protecting your family, though of course they may try to if push comes to shove. The goal is to have the dog bring your attention to something, hopefully giving you enough time to take appropriate action.

Recommended breeds for watch dog duty include most of the terriers. They are alert, loyal, and tend to bark fiercely at anyone or anything they perceive to be a threat or to be invading their territory. Other suitable breeds are poodles, Chihuahuas, miniature schnauzers, and dachshunds.

Owning one of these breeds can mean putting up with nuisance barking. While some dogs can have this trained out of them, it is often an arduous process. Like the story about the boy who cried wolf, an owner who has put up with nuisance barking for several months or years will tend to ignore all but the most fervent alerts the dog gives. To a degree, you have to take the good with the bad. The best suggestion I can give is to work daily with training your dog and get to know their differing barks. As any dog owner will tell you, a dog's barks can be as different as a baby's cries, with each tone or pattern having a distinct meaning.

GUARD DOGS

These are the elite soldiers compared to the watch dog security guards. Think of the difference like this: A watch dog will tell you about danger, whereas a guard dog is going to do something about it. Therefore, in addition to possessing high intelligence and a good temperament, a guard dog is also typically a larger animal with enough muscle to get the job done.

One thing to consider about guard dogs is the amount of training they require. This entails a considerable investment of time and resources and not a small amount of risk. The necessary training should be done through a reputable company and is not something the average dog owner can do on their own.

Often, an animal fully trained as a guard dog cannot also be a "family dog." It can be just too difficult for some canines to differentiate between the two roles, which puts family members, particularly young children, at risk. It is for this reason that I usually refrain from suggesting that families invest in an actual guard dog. However, there are several dog breeds that naturally move to physically protect their "pack" and have the muscle to back that up while at the same time are welcome additions to homes with children. In my opinion, most people will be best served by owning a dog that has natural protective instincts rather than one that has been extensively trained to attack.

GERMAN SHEPHERD German shepherds rank near the top of any list of guard dog breeds. They are intelligent, loyal, and can be fiercely protective. Another advantage they have over some other breeds is that they are calm in the face of chaos. Shepherds also tend to remain somewhat detached when dealing with non-family members. By that, I mean they often will not be swayed by overt attempts to be friendly to them. Shepherds have a strong desire to feel useful and don't do well in an environment where they aren't given things to do. Due to their curious nature, they are often trained as search dogs in addition to their work pulling guard duty.

ROTTWEILLER Rottweillers make excellent guard dogs. They are strong, smart, and protective. While much maligned in recent years due to their use in guarding drug houses, they make exceptional family pets. Like the German shepherd, they generally couldn't care less about a stranger attempting to befriend them and instead will concentrate on protecting the family. Rotts are very self-assured and confident, as well as courageous. They have an innate desire to protect their families due to being genetically predisposed as guard animals.

BULLMASTIFF The bullmastiff is a very large dog, no two ways about it, reaching well over 100 pounds at adulthood. As should be evident from their size, they are tremendously strong. Bullmastiffs are also extremely intelligent and alert. They are great with children, as long as you bear in mind the size difference between the dog

MY OWN DOGS

One of the best dogs I've ever owned was a beloved Siberian husky named Nikita. She was very protective of her "pack." When our kids were little, Nikita made a point every single night to go into each of their rooms to check on them before she'd lay down to sleep. She'd go right up to their beds and sniff around to ensure all was well. If for some reason she didn't have access to the room, such as a baby gate being up across the doorway, she'd sit and wait until we let her in.

An interesting tidbit about huskies (and other blue-eyed animals) is that they have a red eye-shine. At night, when light hits their eyes and where other animals would show a greenish or yellowish glow, theirs are red. This can be decidedly disconcerting to someone who isn't expecting it. In fact, the first time my wife noticed it, she called me at work and jokingly said our dog was possessed!

Another breed that I know from personal experience makes a great watch dog is a keeshond. They were originally bred as Dutch boat dogs and have two coats. The outer coat is very long, yet they shed very little. The inner coat is extremely soft and serves to keep them warm even when wet. Keeshonds are very loyal to their owners. While they tend to be a bit friendlier than other recommended watch dogs, their alertness makes up for it, in my opinion. Our keeshond Harley was always on the lookout for anything amiss and made sure we knew when he saw something. He was also keenly aware of our moods, and when things weren't going right, he always tried to comfort us as best he could.

and the child. What could be meant as nothing more than a playful swat with a paw could send a child sprawling. One downside of the bullmastiff is that they tend not to get along well with other dogs. They were bred to work independently as well as to guard against canine intruders, so they are predisposed to have issues with other dogs in the home.

DOBERMAN PINSCHER Doberman pinschers also rank high on the list of guard dog breeds. They consistently hit high marks in canine intelligence, usually ranking within the top five breeds in any study. They have also been found to have very low aggression toward their owners and families, with relatively high aggression toward strangers. Dobermans are strong and agile, as well as extremely fast runners. They are extremely loyal, good-natured, and very trainable.

Bear in mind that while there are many breeds that historically make great guard dogs, canines are as individual as people. We may know the Mayans as brilliant mathematicians but I'm willing to bet there were at least a few of them who couldn't count to twenty-one without dropping their shorts. Likewise, you may find yourself owning a German shepherd that through some genetic quirk happens to have low intelligence. This is why it is important, if purchasing a purebred dog, to visit the breeder's facilities and see the parents of the puppy you are selecting. However, if you still end up with a dog that doesn't quite meet your expectations, I am of the strong opinion that owning a dog is a lifetime commitment. Unless there is a genuine safety issue, the dog deserves to have a home where it is welcome, regardless of capabilities. Just like people, dogs can surprise you by performing admirably when it would be least expected.

Training

Whether you are considering a guard dog, a watch dog, or just a canine companion, they all need at least a modicum of training. Your dog should know, at a minimum, basic commands like sit, stay, come, and heel. As you progress through the training, you'll also want to teach your dog to stop barking once you are alerted to a problem. Doing so will allow you to concentrate on the problem at hand without being distracted by continued barking. Furthermore, there might very well be a time when it will be imperative for your dog to remain quiet.

QUIET COMMAND

One way to teach the "quiet" command is the following. Every time your dog barks, tell it to be quiet, then call the dog over to you. Reward it immediately with praise and a small treat. Keep at it and soon the dog will develop a habit or even a reflex of barking, then going directly to a family member. This, like any other command training, may take time to develop. In the beginning, it may be difficult to get the dog to stop barking long enough to hear and recognize a command to be quiet. If that's the case, use what trainers call an interrupter. This is a device you can make yourself that will create noise and momentarily distract the dog. It can be as simple as a soda can with a few pebbles in it. If your dog is barking incessantly and won't respond to you, shake the can briefly.

With the "quiet" command in particular, it is important the command be given in an even and firm tone of voice. Trying to shout over the dog's noise may cause it to think you are "barking" right along with it. The end result is just more noise from both of you, with nothing accomplished.

RELEASE COMMAND

Don't forget to teach your dog a release word. This is the command you'll give when the dog has completed the tasks you've instructed it to do. For example, if you tell your dog to sit and stay, obviously at some point the dog should be released from those commands. When choosing a release word, use something that makes sense to you but is not something that would likely come up in every day conversation, such as "OK." The reason I mention this is, let's say you put your dog in the sit/stay command while you're talking to your spouse. He asks you how work was today and you reply, "It was OK." The dog hears that and figures it has been released from the sit/stay, even though you weren't even looking at it.

I highly discourage people from trying to teach their dogs to attack. It can be very difficult to do this effectively without having first received proper training in it yourself. Going it alone on something like that is running a big risk that your dog will bite a family member or an innocent visitor to your home. Given that such occurrences can bring criminal charges to the dog owner in many areas of the country, it is something you should work hard to avoid.

CHAPTER 11
Communications

The ability to send and receive information may prove to be absolutely crucial to your post-collapse survival. We currently live in an age where we enjoy almost instant communication with people all over the globe. After a collapse, much of that convenience will likely disappear, but we'll still need to be able to communicate effectively with not only our immediate team members but also hopefully at least the local world around us.

While we'll no longer be able to pull up weather reports from halfway across the planet in a heartbeat, we might be able to find out that the village an hour west of us just experienced a horrendous storm that is now headed east at a good clip. And it would truly be beneficial to learn that a group of Mutant Zombie Bikers just passed through the town to the north and is headed in our direction, wouldn't it?

In this chapter we'll explore some of the methods of communication that might still be available to you in a post-collapse scenario. Keep in mind that all of the devices discussed need power to operate. You will be well served by investing in a couple of small solar panel arrays that allow you to charge batteries and small electronics. While a couple hundred dollars sounds like a steep investment just to run small gadgets, the ability to continue using your communication equipment will be invaluable.

Shortwave Radio

Shortwave radios are relatively inexpensive, compared to their value both now and post-collapse. They will allow you to listen to broadcasts from across town as well as across the globe.

These are strictly information-gathering devices, as you obviously won't be using them to transmit. Many survivalists agree they get a much more impartial newscast

by listening to the programs from overseas than they do from our domestic stations. In the event of some sort of disaster that is centered on North America, many of those stations, such as the BBC out of the UK, will still be broadcasting. You can also use shortwave radios to listen in on ham radio broadcasts, which we'll discuss shortly.

Radio Scanner

I have long advocated the purchase of a portable radio scanner, sometimes referred to as a police scanner. While it might end up having little value in the wake of a collapse, a scanner could prove to be utterly priceless in the

PHONETIC ALPHABETS

To avoid any misunderstandings when spelling names or other words, law enforcement and other agencies will often use one of the common phonetic alphabets. This prevents confusion between similar-sounding letters like B and D. In the U.S., there are two main alphabets, one used by military agencies and the other by law enforcement. Naturally, there may be local variations on these alphabets.

LETTER	MILITARY/AVIATION	LAW ENFORCEMENT
A	Alpha	Adam
B	Bravo	Boy
C	Charlie	Charles
D	Delta	David
E	Echo	Edward
F	Foxtrot	Frank
G	Golf	George
H	Hotel	Henry
I	India	Ida
J	Juliet	John
K	Kilo	King
L	Lima	Lincoln
M	Mike	Mary
N	November	Nora
O	Oscar	Ocean
P	Papa	Peter
Q	Quebec	Queen
R	Romeo	Robert
S	Sierra	Sam
T	Tango	Tom
U	Uniform	Union
V	Victor	Victor
W	Whiskey	William
X	X-ray	X-ray
Y	Yankee	Young
Z	Zulu	Zebra

days leading up to and immediately following a disaster.

A radio scanner allows you to listen in on radio traffic transmitted by the police, fire departments, rescue squads, and any number of other official and even unofficial agencies. To use the scanner, you'll need to determine the correct frequencies to program into the unit. This information is easily found online as well as in regularly published books that are usually sold right alongside the scanners in stores like Radio Shack.

Most scanners organize the frequencies into banks. For example, a four-hundred-channel radio scanner will typically have ten banks, each containing up to forty different channels or frequencies. This allows you to fully customize the scanner for your specific needs. You could set up Bank 1 to be for all local law enforcement agencies, Bank 2 for all the local fire departments, and so on. Don't forget state and federal agencies as well.

The idea here is to gather intelligence by listening to the activities of law enforcement and other agencies. They will all be surely using radios right up until the radios become useless. Officers will be communicating with each other as well as their dispatch center. Dispatchers will be relaying information to the officers in the field. All of this information going back and forth will be valuable. You'll be able to learn which stores may still be in business and which ones have been looted, which areas of the county to avoid at all costs due to riots and other unpleasantness,

POLICE 10 CODES

Back in 1937, when police radio traffic was limited by the small number of available channels, Charles "Charlie" Hopper was Communications Director for the Illinois State Police. He is credited with being the person who invented the now-popular "10 Code" method for police radio communication. The intention was to create something of a shorthand for officers to use on the radio. Soon, the use of these 10 Codes became standard among law enforcement agencies across the United States.

While the meaning of some of these codes varies between jurisdictions, most of the more commonly used ones, such as 10-4 and 10-20, are similar across the board. After spending some time listening to the transmissions in your area, you'll begin to learn the local meanings of any variances from the following standard codes. In very recent years, many jurisdictions have moved back to using plain speech instead of the codes. However, you'll still hear many of these codes being used by the more experienced officers.

10-0 Caution
10-1 Unable to copy transmission
10-2 Signal good/strong
10-3 Stop transmitting
10-4 Acknowledgment (OK)
10-5 Relay
10-6 Busy
10-7 Out of service
10-8 In service
10-9 Repeat
10-10 Fight in progress
10-11 Dog case
10-12 Stand by (stop)
10-13 Weather or traffic report

10-14 Prowler report
10-15 Civil disturbance
10-16 Domestic disturbance
10-17 Meet complainant
10-18 Quickly
10-19 Return to [location]
10-20 Location
10-21 Call [person] by telephone
10-22 Disregard
10-23 Arrived at scene
10-24 Assignment completed
10-25 Meet with [person]
10-26 Detaining subject
10-27 Driver's license information

Communications

10-28 Vehicle registration information
10-29 Check for warrants
10-30 Unnecessary use of radio
10-31 Crime in progress
10-32 Man with gun
10-33 Emergency
10-34 Riot
10-35 Major crime alert
10-36 Correct time
10-37 Suspicious vehicle
10-38 Stopping suspicious vehicle
10-39 Urgent: use light, siren
10-40 Silent run: no light, siren
10-41 Beginning tour of duty
10-42 Ending tour of duty
10-43 Information
10-44 Permission to leave
10-45 Animal carcass
10-46 Assist motorist
10-47 Emergency road repairs
10-48 Traffic standard repair
10-49 Traffic light out at ...
10-50 Traffic accident
10-51 Wrecker needed
10-52 Ambulance needed
10-53 Road blocked
10-54 Livestock on highway
10-55 Suspected DUI
10-56 Intoxicated pedestrian
10-57 Hit and run
10-58 Direct traffic
10-59 Convoy or escort
10-60 Squad in vicinity
10-61 Personnel in vicinity
10-62 Reply to message
10-63 Prepare to make written copy

10-64 Message for local delivery
10-65 Net message assignment
10-66 Message cancellation
10-67 Clear for net message
10-68 Dispatch information
10-69 Message received
10-70 Fire
10-71 Advise nature of fire
10-72 Report progress on fire
10-73 Smoke report
10-74 Negative
10-75 In contact with [person]
10-76 En route to [location]
10-77 Estimated time of arrival (ETA)
10-78 Need assistance
10-79 Notify coroner
10-80 Chase in progress
10-81 Breathalyzer
10-82 Reserve lodging
10-83 Work school crossing
10-84 If meeting, advise ETA
10-85 Delayed due to [reason]
10-86 Officer/operator on duty
10-87 Pick up/distribute checks
10-88 Present telephone number
10-89 Bomb threat
10-90 Bank alarm
10-91 Pick up prisoner/subject
10-92 Improperly parked vehicle
10-93 Blockade
10-94 Drag racing
10-95 Prisoner/subject in custody
10-96 Mental subject
10-97 Check (test) signal
10-98 Prison/jail break
10-99 Wanted/stolen indicated

and perhaps most importantly, which agencies are still working and which ones have given it up as a bad job.

I advise you to get a portable scanner, rather than a desktop model. This way, if your plan in the event of a major disaster or crisis is to evacuate your immediate area and travel to another retreat location, you can program your scanner with the frequencies used by law enforcement in each of the localities you'll travel through or between home and your retreat. As you travel, you can tune in to these channels to hopefully get a heads-up on coming roadblocks or other situations before you get to them. It will be difficult to do this with a tabletop radio scanner. Be sure you have extra batteries available to you in your travels.

Ham Radio

Even if society has fully disintegrated and all is chaos, odds are pretty good there will still be ham radio operators transmitting. There are countless stories through recent history showing not only the innovation of these folks but their perseverance. They can make an antenna out of darn near anything and many of them are already using solar cells to power their equipment.

As mentioned earlier, you can pull in ham radio transmissions on a decent shortwave radio, but you won't be able to transmit. While one-way communication is usually preferable to none at all, you'd be well advised to invest in a good, basic ham radio setup. The expense isn't too great, especially if you find it used at a ham swap meet.

Bear in mind that it is illegal to transmit over the radio without being duly licensed. Post-collapse, I doubt there will be an FCC at all, let alone people going around triangulating radio signals to bust unlicensed activity. But I always stress the importance of staying legal as long as there are laws around to follow.

Also, ham radio communication is something you will want to practice while you have the benefit of many mentors, teachers, and advisors available to you. This isn't a case of buying the equipment and just mothballing it until and unless it is ever truly needed. Obtaining the license isn't a big deal or a huge expense, and it will allow you to use your gear legally.

Once you have your basic rig set up and your license is hanging on the wall, get to know the ham operators in your area. Many of them are preppers, even if they don't identify themselves as such. Most of them are well trained in emergency communication in addition to weather spotting. I have yet to meet a ham radio operator who won't bend over backwards to help out someone new to the field. Communicate with local hams regularly, go to ham swap meets in your area, and join the clubs available to you. These things will help you increase your overall knowledge about ham radio operation. Also, by letting hams in your area get to know you, once the collapse happens, they'll hopefully recognize you on the air and be more willing to communicate with you. Remember, a friendly face (or perhaps voice in this case) now will help thaw the ice a bit down the road, should the need arise.

WHAT RADIO SHOULD I GET?
by Don Jones

There are a lot of used ham radios for sale but not just any radio will do. Always do your own homework. What is your budget? What do you want the radio for? If you want to talk across town to a buddy, then you do not want to get an HF radio but a two-meter radio. There is a big difference between the two. With HF radios, you can talk to someone several hundred miles away or even around the world. If you try to talk with some one across town who also has an HF, then you are just too close to each other. HF is for long-distance communications.

Two-meter radios are generally used in what is called line of sight communications. The radio goes to another radio nearby or hits a repeater that picks up the signal and then boosts it so it will go to another tower. This way you can get distance on a small radio.

When you buy on the web, "Let the buyer beware." Do your homework. Check out the sales history of the seller. Ask a lot of questions. Does it come with a wiring harness? Does it have a microphone? Is it a tube-type radio (which beginners should avoid)? Has it been modified?

Also, be alert that some folks sell radios and have no clue about how they work. If the seller says they turned the

Communicating Within the Group

Another aspect of security communications is the need to stay in touch with your team members, whether they are patrolling the immediate area or sent off on local scouting or scavenging missions. For portable communications, radio on and it lit up but they heard nothing, the question to ask is did they put an antenna on it? If so, was it the right kind of antenna? Did it have a built-in speaker? Or does it require an external speaker?

Also, ask a local ham who has nothing to sell you or to gain what they think about that particular radio. If the ham is a good friend, they just might be able to steer you clear of a bad sale. Another thing to think about is if you purchase a radio that you are told does not work and it is for parts, it might be to your advantage to buy it and send it back to the factory for repair. Compared to the cost to a new radio, you will most likely come out a winner.

Donald Jones is a retired minister and has worked with the Red Cross as an instructor of CPR, First Aid, Communicable Disease, Wilderness First Aid, Pet First Aid and Disaster Preparedness. He has been involved with amateur radio for several years and has served as a Red Cross hurricane shelter ham operator during Hurricanes Charley, Francis, Wilma, and Ivan. He is a member of Amateur Radio Emergency Services (ARES) of Marin County, Florida, and has written for QST Magazine *about the hurricane experiences. He has become known as the Amateur Radio Survivalist and can be found online on Facebook administrating the Amateur Radio Survivalist group.*

there are two basic radio options: Family Radio Service (FRS) and General Mobile Radio Service (GMRS). While Citizen's Band (CB) radio equipment still remains popular among many people, it is often subject to interference and thus not really reliable for our purposes. With that said, should you find used CB equipment in good condition at

an affordable price, it wouldn't be the worst idea to have
it on hand just for listening purposes.

GENERAL MOBILE RADIO SERVICE

General Mobile Radio Service (GMRS) equipment requires
an FCC license to operate under current laws. Obtaining
a license is simply a matter of filling out an application
and paying a fee. There is no exam required. The license

CODE WORDS

The lack of privacy when using radios for communication
brings up the topic of codes. This may sound like a bit of
cloak-and-dagger stuff. But if your life, and the lives of your
family, depend upon reliable yet covert communication, the
use of code words and phrases may be prudent. Another
advantage of using codes is the ability to transmit a clearly
understood message with a minimum of words.

The critical elements of using codes are, first, that
everyone involved knows what the codes mean, and
second, that everyone agrees to use the codes in all radio
communications. For example, let's say you've agreed the
use of the word "red" will always mean there is immediate
danger. One day post-collapse, one member of your team is
conducting a routine check of the perimeter and comments
on the radio that the sunset "...sure looks red tonight." Are
they making reference to having seen danger to the west
or are they really just commenting on the color of the sky?
It needs to be understood among every single member of
the team or family that the code words selected can only be
used as code words when communicating over the radio. This

will cover the primary licensee as well as the licensee's immediate family.

GMRS radios operate on a line-of-sight basis, with optimal conditions allowing for communication of up to a couple miles. Because they are line of sight, the higher the transmitter is, the farther the signal will reach. So, for example, someone transmitting from the roof of a two-story home will be able to transmit a longer distance than

---

is why phrases often work better than individual words as codes. If your team member says the sunset is red tonight, no big deal. But if she says, "Good hunting tonight, just saw several badgers to the west," then batten down the hatches, as trouble is on the way.

Incidentally, the use of codes can extend to the time before a collapse. I know several preppers who have instituted the use of code phrases to be sent via text or email to their family members in the event of an emergency. These include:

Code Red   Come home immediately. Do not pass Go, do not collect $200. Just get your butt home as fast as possible.

Monkey Butt   Danger is imminent, seek shelter wherever you are immediately. Once shelter is achieved, call for more information if possible.

5 x 5   All OK here, waiting for more information.

The use of codes like these before a collapse allows you to communicate with your family and team members quickly when they need to take immediate action.

CHANNELS

This chart shows the channels and frequencies used by GRMS and FRS radios.

CHANNEL	TYPE	FREQUENCY
1	FRS and GMRS	462.5625
2	FRS and GMRS	462.5875
3	FRS and GMRS	462.6125
4	FRS and GMRS	462.6375
5	FRS and GMRS	462.6625
6	FRS and GMRS	462.6875
7	FRS and GMRS	462.7125
8	FRS	467.5625
9	FRS	467.5875
10	FRS	467.6125
11	FRS	467.6375
12	FRS	467.6625
13	FRS	467.6875
14	FRS	467.7125
15	GMRS	462.5500
16	GMRS	462.5750
17	GMRS	462.6000
18	GMRS	462.6250
19	GMRS	462.6500
20	GMRS	462.6750
21	GMRS	462.7000
22	GMRS	462.7250

someone standing on the ground, all other factors being equal. This is something to keep in mind as you plan out your security communications plan. If you choose to use any line-of-sight radio equipment, consider stationing someone in an elevated position in order to pull in stronger signals.

GMRS radios are typically small, handheld units, very much like the walkie-talkies many of us played with as kids. They will transmit on fifteen different channels, the first seven of which are shared with Family Radio Service (FRS). The remaining eight channels are reserved exclusively for GMRS.

FAMILY RADIO SERVICE

Family Radio Service (FRS) units also operate on line of sight, but the effective range is considerably shorter than GMRS, typically well under a mile. However, the FRS radios don't require a license and are usually more inexpensive.

Again, as with the GMRS radios, they are small units and operate using a couple AA or AAA batteries. They may work well within the retreat's immediate area but 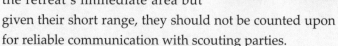 given their short range, they should not be counted upon for reliable communication with scouting parties.

There are seven channels devoted to FRS communications, with an additional eight that are shared with GMRS. These shared channels allow for communication between the two different types of equipment. You can also get hybrid units that operate on both GMRS and FRS channels.

While pricey when compared to FRS units, they are likely to be worth the expense. There are twenty-two channels total between FRS and GMRS radios and these combined units will allow you to use all of them.

Bear in mind that with both of these types of units, the communications are in no way private. Anyone with similar equipment, or even just a radio scanner, can tune in and listen to the conversations. This has caused more than a few families great frustration when they've taken their brand new FRS units to the county fair or other big event, planning to use them to communicate among the family members. After turning the units on, they are inundated with conversations going on constantly on most of the channels.

If you've take my earlier advice to purchase a radio scanner, you might consider programming in the frequencies for GMRS and FRS channels. Doing so will allow you to eavesdrop on anyone using these devices in your immediate area and possibly get a heads-up on what might be headed your way.

CHAPTER 12
Mutual Aid Agreements

Despite how often the old adage "There's no 'i' in the word 'team' " gets tossed around, we tend to concentrate more on individual achievement than team accomplishment. Even a cursory glance through the list of the most popular action movies will readily show that we as a culture delight in seeing the underdog succeed. The *Rambo* series, the *Die Hard* movies, the list goes on and on; all concentrate on an individual overcoming ever-more-ridiculous odds to win.

As a result, we have ingrained into our society the belief that the individual is often more important than the team. This has, of course, seeped into survivalist culture as much as anywhere else. If you spend much time at all perusing various online forums or reading survival manuals, you'll see example after example of what I call Lone Wolf Syndrome.

Lone Wolf Syndrome

"Lone Wolf Syndrome" is a term I coined a few years ago. It refers to the general mindset of a survivalist who plans to just head for the hills at the first sign of trouble and live out the remainder of their days all on their own with no support system, just them against the world. I'll agree that this plan will work to the degree that the survivalist in question may indeed live out the rest of their life on their own. But the rest of their life probably won't be nearly as long as they think.

Survivalists with this sort of plan will point to the much-vaunted mountain men of the American Old West as the ideal they wish to emulate. These trailblazers and trappers would indeed spend long periods of time all on their own in the wild. However, those suffering from Lone Wolf Syndrome are quick to forget a couple other facts about mountain men:

The lifespan of the average mountain man was relatively short. Many of them lasted only several years out in the wild, rather than anything close to the decades Hollywood and fiction would have us believe.

Far from living completely solitary lives, mountain men regularly visited towns to stock up on supplies. While there, they'd likely visit saloons and other businesses. They also frequently worked in groups on their trapping runs. Many of them befriended Native American tribes and even married some of their women. These tribes would let the mountain men stay with them for long periods of time.

Human beings are social animals. That's just how we're wired as a species. Sure, there are plenty of people out there who by either choice or conditioning live solitary lives. Many of them will insist they are never lonely and just prefer their own company. They are the exception rather than the rule. One of the most basic needs a person has is a sense of love and belonging. This need is typically met through family relationships, friendships, and sexual intimacy.

Remember, there is a reason why solitary confinement is considered a severe punishment. The human mind craves interaction with others and when this is denied for even moderate lengths of time, it can lead to depression and even semi-permanent changes to brain physiology.

Mutual Aid Agreements

The point here is that planning to go it all alone is planning to fail, whether you're talking about heading for the hills or barricading yourself inside a home or retreat forever. Sooner or later, you'll need to sleep, eat, use the toilet, tend to crops, or any other of a hundred different activities that will call your immediate attention away from security concerns. If you plan to have a family or small group at your retreat with you, then many of those concerns will be addressed by rotating shifts of patrols, lookouts, and other security details.

There is also great value in networking with your immediate neighbors to form what we'll call mutual aid agreements. The idea behind a mutual aid agreement is that you and the others involved agree to watch over each other and provide assistance as needed, particularly in matters related to security. For example, say that one night post-collapse you observe a few individuals attempting to raid your neighbor's garden. Rather than just turning away from the window, glad it was his garden and not yours, you'd do whatever you could to both alert your neighbor and protect his garden. In return, your neighbor would do the same for you.

Ideally, this sort of agreement would extend to other matters, such as the growing of crops. By sharing the burden of feeding the families, more hands can work larger areas and provide better results. I'm not at all suggesting the families put all their supplies into some sort of common area, free for the taking. What I'm getting at is that by fostering cooperative agreements with your neighbors, you can gain valuable allies. Don't forget those who might not be living immediately next to you either. By getting to know survivalists in your general area, you can not only learn from them but work out mutual aid agreements with them as well. It could be that at some point down the road, you'll learn there is a large group of the ever-popular Mutant Zombie Bikers headed your way and you'll need all the help you can get.

FINDING OTHER PREPPERS

One of the most common complaints I hear from preppers is the difficulty in finding like-minded folks in their area. They feel as though they are lone voices in the wind and struggle to locate anyone nearby who shares their concerns about the future.

Here's the thing. Let's reverse the question for a second and look at it like this: How many people in your area know *you* are a prepper? Not too many, I'd reckon. And that's probably by design, isn't it? The rules of OPSEC dictate that you keep your trap shut and not go around blabbering to people how you have umpteen cases of toilet paper and hundreds of gallons of water stored in the basement. This makes perfect sense. However, the reason you are finding it difficult to find preppers in your area is because *they are all doing the same thing!* They are keeping their heads down and their mouths shut, just like you. The result is, there could be a roomful of preppers and none of them would be aware of it.

Try this at the next informal gathering you attend, such as a lawn party. Obviously TV shows about prepping have been popular for a while now, so pick one that is reasonably current and casually ask if anyone has seen it. Odds are, you'll hear several people confirm they have seen it and they'll follow it up with some sort of derogatory comment about "...the nut jobs who think the world is going to end." During the ensuing conversation, mention how you think it probably isn't a bad idea to have at least some extra food and supplies set aside, "just in case." I'd be willing to bet you'll get at least a few head nods at that. Those nodding are probably preppers or at least people who are interested in it. Those are the folks to get to know better. You may never get to the point where you'd trust them enough to give them a guided tour of your preps. The idea is to find people in your local area who are like-minded when it comes to disaster readiness so that you have folks you could perhaps call upon for assistance down the road, should the need arise.

If there will be one silver lining in the cloud of a post-collapse world, it will be that you no longer will need to try to convince potential allies that they should prepare for the worst. Gone, for the most part, will be endless debates about whether preppers are nutjobs or just forward thinkers. Most people will readily admit that there is strength in numbers. Therefore, it shouldn't take too much conversation to convince the survivors around you that you will all benefit by banding together and watching each others' backs.

EVERYONE HAS VALUE

Don't ever overlook a potential ally because of their physical condition, infirmities, or other negatively perceived attributes. The 90-year-old widow who can hardly walk due to arthritis may have spent several decades of her life growing gardens and be able share that knowledge with you. She may also have been the resident busybody and can tell you at a glance who lives where, how long they've lived there, what they do for a living, and who has been shacking up with them. The guy in a wheelchair may be an excellent shot with a hunting rifle and make one dandy of a sniper. (Just be sure to brace his wheelchair before handing him the rifle. Failure to do so might result in something out of a Bugs Bunny cartoon.) The asthmatic teenager might never win a footrace but may have enough gadget know-how to cobble together one heck of a communications system and man it regularly.

There is a saying that war makes for strange bedfellows. Make no mistake, for at least a period of time following a collapse, it will be as though you are at war with the world at large. Out of necessity, you may find yourself teaming up with neighbors you dislike. As the proverb goes, "The enemy of my enemy is my friend."

NEIGHBORS

Of course, the first people you'd probably consider for a mutual aid agreement would be your immediate neighbors. In an urban environment, this may mean all of the survivors who live in your building and perhaps neighboring buildings. This could possibly amount to several dozen people or more. Out in the sticks, the options are going to be a bit scarcer in many places. While that will result in fewer mouths needing sustenance, it will also mean fewer hands available to work gardens and such.

Either way, though, your neighbors are in a position to provide extra eyes and ears. They know the area and are likely to be able to spot strangers easily. If you haven't done so already, make a point of getting to know your neighbors well. Invite them over for a barbecue in the summer and exchange cookies in December. Organize a floor party in your apartment building. Compliment the owner of the condo next door on their flower boxes. In today's society, we've become rather insular and closed off in our daily lives. This will be nothing but a hindrance in the future.

SURVIVAL COMMUNITIES

Not a week goes by where I don't see a post on one or another online forum from someone looking to join a "survival community." Typically, these people have some sort of pie in the sky ideal in mind. They envision a group of people living together in something akin to an old 1960s-era commune, but with security elements added to the mix.

I hate to break it to you but for the most part, these communities are almost like a prepper urban legend. Sure, there are established groups out there, but they are few and far between. Furthermore, none of them are looking to add new and unknown people to their groups. For the most part, these groups have been together for many years and the members know each other intimately. They have no reason to look outside the group for more folks to join up. OK, so you have an extensive military background and are offering to trade your experience for a place in the group. Guess what? Most of the members of these established groups are also ex-military and they have no need of another mouth to feed.

My best advice to those who are looking to join an established group is to concentrate your efforts and energy elsewhere. With that said, though, should you become aware of a group in your area, there is nothing wrong with trying to set up alliances with them. The groups of which I'm aware are, at least at this point in time, not intending to become some sort of warlord regime in their area after a societal collapse. They are just planning to be able to provide for their own survival, come what may. It could be beneficial to network with members of this type of group and try to work out some sort of agreement with them to assist you in times of need in exchange for extra produce from your gardens or some other commodity.

CHAPTER 13
Children and Security

Let's face it, the reason we prep is to provide for the safety and security of our families, come what may. But, as with any other aspect of life, when you add children to the mix, things get complicated quickly. It is far easier to make plans and implement them if it is just you or you and a spouse. Children, especially young'uns, can create challenges.

Children and OPSEC

As any parent will attest, we spend the first two years of a child's life teaching them to walk and talk, then the next sixteen years or so trying to get them to sit down and be quiet. Most of the time, it is because kids can be loud and obnoxious, often without realizing it. But when we talk about OPSEC, it is crucial for them to be able to keep their mouths shut.

Children need to be taught at an early age that some topics of conversation just aren't discussed outside the home or with people outside the immediate family. Just as your son surely wouldn't want you sharing with folks at the grocery store the fact that you call him "Peanut" around the house, you don't want him telling those same people about the 45 pounds of rice you already have stockpiled as you grab four more bags from a shelf.

As they get older, the challenge shifts a bit to where talking about your preps to strangers isn't as much of a problem as talking to their friends about it. Teenagers have a tendency to disparage much of what adults around them say and do and prepping is no exception. On the other hand, teens—boys especially—are often fascinated by firearms and other weaponry. So while your son might roll his eyes when you walk in the door with yet another case of canned vegetables, he won't think twice about bragging to his buddy how he got to shoot four different rifles at the range Saturday morning.

If you live in a rural area where hunting is popular, that might not be a big deal. However, if you live in the city or suburbs and you're probably the only home in the area that has firearms, then you might want to be concerned about that little tidbit of information having been shared. Personally, I grew up in a very rural part of the country and deer hunting was so popular that the high school would come close to shutting down during rifle season, as there were so many absences. Of course, this was also back when it wasn't uncommon to see rifles in a truck rack in the student parking lot, as there were some students who'd hit the woods right after the last bell rang.

Include Pre-collapse Scenarios in Your Planning

Your planning should include life before a collapse as well. Discuss with your children what they should do if they are approached by a stranger, if they are home alone and someone comes to the door, and how to approach other relatively common dangers. Having the knowledge of how to deal with these types of situations leads to an increase in self-confidence.

Be sure to keep these plans age-appropriate. Telling your four-year-old to kick a threatening stranger in the groin, when they are barely tall enough to be eye to eye with the person's belt buckle, probably isn't going to work very well. At that age, the child should concentrate on screaming and trying to get away from the abductor rather than physically attacking them. Instruct them to yell things like, "He is not my daddy!" while pulling and squirming to get away. The hope is that the abductor will cease his actions and flee, and that people in the area will be able to provide a description of him as well as his vehicle.

In addition to these more run-of-the-mill scenarios, as a prepping family you should also discuss the more major crises. For example, what is the plan if a major event occurs and they are being held at school in a lockdown? Word to the wise with regard to this particular scenario: Spare me the macho crap about how you'd run in and grab your kid from the school, no matter who tries to stop you. You won't be doing your family, or anyone else, much good when you're sitting in the back of a squad car, handcuffed and still twitching from the Tasing you received when you assaulted an officer.

In a situation where your child is in a school lockdown, unless you have a truly compelling reason to believe otherwise, the child is probably safer right where they are. In this day and age, public school staff members are rather well trained on what to do in emergency situations and that training has often been conducted by members of law enforcement, not just a few bean counters from an insurance company. You won't like waiting it out, but unless society is truly collapsing around your eyes, bide your time and try to learn as much as you can about the current situation.

I highly suggest parents get involved with the schools their children attend. Get to know the teachers and staff. Doing so is not just good parenting, it can help when problems crop up. If they know you by face and name, staff members are usually at least a bit more accommodating if you are asking for something that might be a bit out of the ordinary, such as allowing your child to keep a small pack with extra food, water, and such in their classroom.

Find out what the procedures are for various emergencies, such as lockdowns, fire evacuations, and severe weather. By being well informed, you are in a much better position to make rational and well-thought-out decisions, rather than acting rash and emotional.

Communicate Effectively

Remember that children often see and hear far more than we may realize, and it all goes through their own little filters. An offhand comment one night while watching the latest zombie movie can be misinterpreted and internalized, later leading to misunderstandings. For example, one afternoon while I was playing in my backyard as a wee lad, a police officer drove by on patrol. I smiled and waved to him and he waved back. My father made some comment about his taxes paying for the officer's salary and I somehow interpreted it to mean that every time I waved at a police officer, my dad's taxes went up. Look, at all of five years old or so, this made perfect sense to me. My point here is, watch what and how you say things around your children to prevent innocent misunderstandings.

It would be impossible for me to give you any specific age at which a child would be capable of understanding prepping and OPSEC. I've known seven-year-olds who would grasp the basic concepts better than a couple of teenagers I've met. You'll need to gauge the maturity level of each child involved. When they've reached a stage of intellectual and emotional development such that they understand it is wrong for them to take things that belong to others, you can start talking about the need to keep the contents of your pantry private.

Indeed, the discussions should concentrate on keeping things *private*, not secret. Try to avoid couching it in terms of "keeping secrets." The reason for this is that when a child talks about a family keeping secrets, school guidance counselors and staff members are trained to treat that as a red flag. Think about it like this for a second: Let's say you take your family out in the backyard to practice lighting campfires. While trying to use a flint rod, your seven-year-old daughter's hand slips and she gets a small burn mark on her arm from a nearby ember. She goes to school on Monday and the teacher casually asks how she got hurt. At her age, your daughter may have difficulty in distinguishing between not talking about prepping and it being OK to talk about the practice exercise over the weekend. She gets nervous and stammers, "I can't tell you, that's a secret." Want to guess the chain of events that is likely to follow?

Watch the Stress Levels

When you talk with your children about security protocols, watch them carefully for signs of stress and anxiety. It can be an interesting dichotomy: As adults, prepping often tends to calm our worries, securing us in the knowledge that we're taking steps to keep our families safe. Yet, at the same time, discussing with our children how their lives will change in a world without law will often increase their own anxiety levels. Children tend to have very vivid imaginations and having frank conversations with them as to what could happen if everyone doesn't work together as a team on security will put their minds into overdrive.

One of the best things you can do is to be honest with your children. While keeping the discussion age appropriate, don't sugarcoat things. Explain to them that the reason you are making these plans and preparations is to do everything within your power to keep them safe. It is an unfortunate fact that the world has many bad people in it and you want to do whatever you can to keep those bad people away. If you find that your child begins to suffer from bad dreams or seems depressed, please don't ignore or disregard that behavior. Take the time to talk them through their concerns and comfort them as best you can.

Children and Drills

Right in the middle of a sudden crisis is a bad time for children to have to decide the best course of action. This is where drills come in. While we have no way of predicting every possible scenario that may come up post-collapse, we need to determine specific roles to be played by our children within our various security protocols. In some situations, the best action for the child to take may be to head directly to a secure area of the retreat and wait for further instructions. Other scenarios may dictate that the child is to help with relaying information to various family members.

Drills are a way to both practice responses to various scenarios and gauge the abilities of the children. If during a drill the child becomes too flustered to effectively monitor a radio, then I doubt they'd do well in a real situation. However, bear in mind that as time progresses, the child will of course mature and be able to take on more responsibilities.

Practice drills should be performed under a variety of circumstances and made as realistic as is reasonably possible. While having a live fire exercise this coming Saturday afternoon might not work out so well for you, walking around making loud noises and yelling will help inject a fair amount of adrenaline. Post-collapse you'll not want to be making all that much noise, so take advantage of that opportunity now. Make the mistakes now, while the only impact they'll have is the chance to improve your plans, as opposed to later when there may be no "do-overs."

DEALING WITH BULLYING

For as long as there have been children, there have been bullies. I doubt there is anyone reading this who has never once been on the receiving end of bullying. An argument can be made that being bullied is a natural part of growing up. However, it seems as though bullying has changed quite a bit since I was a wee lad on the playground. Today, bullies are as apt to do serious, permanent physical damage as they are to taunt with colorful language.

Teaching your child how to successfully deflect or stop bullying will lead to an increase in self-esteem and self-confidence. Both of these traits are critical for thinking like a survivor. Bullies tend to prey upon those who they feel are weaker than themselves, so the first line of defense, so to speak, is to put out an air of confidence. If a child causes the bully to believe their behavior will lead to injury or at least make them look bad in front of their peers, they'll likely as not seek a different target.

It certainly isn't politically correct to suggest this, but I've always believed the best solution to being bullied is to sock the bully in the nose. It is usually very unexpected and does the job quite well. When one of my sons was young, he was having trouble with a bully. He went through the official

Some examples of drills to conduct include:

EVACUATION   Give the family, including yourself, a very short period of time to assemble at a certain location within the home, ready to walk out the door. Stress the inclusion of each person's bug-out bag as well as having everyone fully dressed. My wife and I, along with our

channels by reporting it to his teacher and other staff but nothing changed. He was reluctant to respond physically as he was afraid he'd be the one who got in trouble, which of course is what the staff members told all students about fighting. I finally called a meeting with his teacher, the principal, the vice-principal, and the guidance counselor. As I recall, the conversation went something like this:

> *Principal:* "Mr. Cobb, we understand your concerns. Do you have any suggestions as to how to deal with the situation?"
>
> *Me:* "I've told my son that the very next time [bully's name] touches him or even so much as looks at him cross-eyed, he is to punch him. If he gets up, he's to punch him again. This will continue until he stays down. Maybe [bully's name] will get it through his head then."
>
> *Principal:* "I don't think we can condone that!"
>
> *Me:* "You're misunderstanding me. I'm not asking for your permission here. I'm just telling you ahead of time exactly what is going to happen. If you want a different course of events, then I'd suggest you step up your efforts to keep [bully's name] away from my son and under control."

Perhaps not too surprisingly, we didn't have problems with the bully again.

three young children, can do this is under three minutes. Can you beat that?

INTRUDERS IN THE HOME   Spring this one on them late at night or in the very early morning hours. Someone has been seen or heard in the house! Who is supposed to go where and do what?

INCOMING BANDITS   A patrolling member of your group has returned in a hurry, saying he saw several ne'er-do-wells headed toward the retreat. Who mans the lookout post? Who distributes weapons and ammo?

Children and Discipline

The unfortunate reality is that, in a world without the rule of law, parents will, out of necessity, need to be much more strict with their children, at least until things have settled down a bit. Kids will need to understand that when they are given an instruction, it will need to be followed immediately and precisely. If Mom yells, "Get down!" the children should hit the ground without hesitation. You can work on that reflex action when you do the drills we discussed earlier.

By "discipline," I'm not only referring to giving time outs for misbehavior either. I'm also talking about things like noise discipline. While we'd still strive for some form of enjoyable childhood for our youngsters in a post-collapse world, they'll need to understand that things have changed. Gone will be the days when they were able to just run amok outside for hours on end without a care for how much noise they made. Without the background noise from vehicles and such, the noise of a few kids screaming and laughing in a backyard will be heard for quite a ways. This may not be a huge deal, depending on the overall circumstances, but it is something to keep in mind.

CHAPTER 14
Bugging Out

In spite of all your best efforts, advance planning, and extensive prepping, you may find yourself in a situation that you and your family are unable to deal with. It could be an attacking force that is too large or determined. Or perhaps a fire breaks out in your home and spreads too quickly for you to handle.

For any number of reasons, you may need to evacuate or "bug out." Obviously you will not be able to take all of your stockpiled supplies with you. However, with a bit of planning, you can arrange to get away with more than just the shirts on your backs.

Bug-Out Planning

The first step in planning to bug out is to determine where you'll go. Survivalists like to use the "Rule of Threes," as often discussed by survivalist guru Ragnar Benson. This rule basically states that you should always have three ways to accomplish a given goal. In this case, you should decide on at least three different locations to which you can evacuate.

Ideally, these will be in opposite directions from your home or retreat. If you are attacked from the north, and your only bug-out destination is also to the north, you've put yourself in quite a pickle. Also, your bug-out locations should not be as close as across the road or down the block. You want to put some serious distance between yourself and your attackers; coming back the next morning to wreak vengeance upon them is nothing more than pure Hollywood fantasy. That said, bugging out to a location that is 300 miles away is a non-starter. Most people are not now, nor will they likely ever be, in good enough physical condition to reasonably consider walking anything close to that far.

The absolute ideal situation for a bug out would be to choose a spot at least a few miles away and stock it with food, water, and gear well ahead of time. These supplies would be well protected and hidden from prying eyes, just waiting for you to arrive. The reality, though, is that few families could afford to fully stock a secondary location, and there is no way to guarantee that no one will ever stumble across your bug-out spot.

Still, planning ahead will better your chances of bugging out successfully, and in the following sections you'll get some tips to help you plan.

LOCATION PLANNING

Here is an example of what I feel would be a reasonable bug-out plan. Your home or retreat is your primary location, of course. Then, you've made arrangements with a like-minded buddy to store some supplies at his family farm about 10 miles away to the north. You've also come to a similar agreement with a family member about 12 miles to the southeast. Finally, you are familiar with a sizable yet little-known park in the middle of nowhere, about 16 miles away to the west. For the two landowners who you have an agreement with, you also agree that, of course, they are welcome to head to your place if they need to bug out, and you will store some of their supplies at your location. You might not be able to store much in the way of supplies at the park, but in all three instances you can also make use of caches we discussed in a previous chapter.

Remember that bugging isn't necessarily going to be your long-term solution. It is merely a place where you can regroup, take stock of the overall situation, and catch your breath for a few days.

Travel Plan

The next element of bug-out planning is to determine how you will get there. Post-collapse, you may not have the option of using a motorized vehicle. Depending on how long it has been since the initial collapse, fuel might have gone bad or just be plain nonexistent. If you do have access to a working car or truck, all the better, but don't count on it.

You should work out at least three different routes to each location (remember the Rule of Threes). These routes should avoid all cities, towns, and villages if at all possible. Pay particular attention to routes that would force you to cross bridges, and consider the fact that those bridges might have either collapsed or been deliberately destroyed. Remember too that if you are on foot, you are not necessarily limited to roadways when traveling. You may be able to take shortcuts through wilderness areas like state parks.

CHOOSING A BUG-OUT BAG

The most common type of bug-out bag is a simple backpack. Make sure each backpack is fitted to the user and is comfortable to wear for long periods of time. While a cheap school backpack would work in a pinch, it's better to get a pack that is designed for hiking and has padded shoulder straps and an adjustable waist. I do not recommend rolling suitcases as bug-out bags, despite how common this idea seems to be online. Using them obviously requires you to travel with one hand occupied at all times and they won't work very well in rough terrain.

The average adult in reasonable physical condition can carry a pack that is about a quarter of their body weight. You can adjust this up or down depending on physical fitness, infirmities, and other factors. Once you have the bug-out bag fully packed, spend a fair amount of time carrying it around to get used to the weight. Obviously, no matter how physically fit you are, the lighter the bag, the better. In my experience, when creating their first bug-out bag, most people tend to include way too much stuff. Start with just the bare basics and see if the bag will be comfortable to wear for extended periods of time. Only then should you consider adding extra goodies.

Along with the routes you'll take to your locations, you should also plan out how you'll leave your actual home or retreat. If your evacuation is due to fire or other natural disaster, it won't matter much which route you take as long as everyone makes it out safely. However, if you are bugging out due to attack, you'll likely want to be able to "exit stage left" as inconspicuously as possible.

If you have the means to do so, consider constructing some sort of rabbit hole that would allow your group to discreetly leave the structure—for example, a concealed route from your safe room to a detached garage or outbuilding. An underground passageway would be ideal, but only if properly constructed. Otherwise, you could create an aboveground path concealed with piles of brush or other debris. If that is not feasible in your situation, at the least plan out different exit strategies ahead of time.

Bug-Out Bags

If you were to search Google for "bug-out bag list," at last count you'd receive about 268,000 hits. Putting together a bug-out bag has become almost a rite of passage for a prepper. Often, it is one of the first things a budding survivalist does.

Traditionally, the bug-out bag is a portable survival kit that is designed to get you from work or another location to your home in relative safety. It is essentially

PACKING TIPS

As you pack the contents into the bug-out bag, whenever feasible use zip-top bags or other means to keep things at least somewhat waterproof. Down the road, those plastic bags can serve a dual purpose in collecting water if needed. Keep the weight in the bag distributed evenly and avoid making the pack top heavy. You'll want to pack frequently used items toward the top of the pack. Ideally the pack will have several outer pockets to help you keep your gear organized.

a tool to take you from a position of weakness (on the road, separated from your family and/or retreat group) to a position of strength (your home or retreat). However, in this instance where you are bugging out FROM your home, you are moving from a position of strength to a position of relative weakness. That being the case, you'll want to stack the deck as best you can.

You may find it prudent to first determine the contents of your bug-out bag, then find a suitable pack to contain it all. If you procure the bag first, you may get something larger than you truly need and feel compelled to fill it to capacity, rendering it too heavy to be practical. On the other hand, a bag that is too small will force you to eliminate potentially vital supplies or gear.

A bug-out bag should be assembled for every person in your family or group. While overlap of many items is desired, so as to provide for extras in the event some things are used up or lost, each bag should also be somewhat customized for the user. This is a great way to get family members involved in preparedness planning. By adding personal items to their bug-out bags, they will develop a sense of ownership.

There are six basic categories of needs that should be met by the contents of a bug-out bag:

1. Water and water filtration
2. Food
3. Shelter
4. Fire-making
5. First aid and hygiene
6. Security

In the following sections, we'll look at each of these one by one.

WATER AND WATER FILTRATION

Under ideal conditions, the human body can survive about three days without water. A bug out will certainly classify as a situation that is less than ideal. You'll not only want to carry water with you but have the means to purify more as you travel.

Most people are probably capable of carrying at least two liters of water without causing too much strain. I suggest that you divide this between two one-liter bottles. This way, once you've emptied the first bottle, you can use it to purify water while you have potable water in the second bottle. A product I particularly like for portable water purification is the Go Berkey Kit, available at www .Directive21.com. It will purify a quart of water at a time, which is just a hair less than a liter. When configured with the Black Berkey filter element, it will purify well over a gallon an hour. The entire unit fits easily into a bug-out bag.

Another option for purification is to purchase specially designed water bottles with the filters built in. These do work well and don't take up any more space than regular water bottles. The downside is that they purify the water as you suck it through the straw, and thus you can't use them to purify water in bulk for cooking. You could also use water purification tablets, though many of them give the water sort of an off taste. Boiling is the absolute best way to purify water, but in a bug-out situation you can't count on having the luxury of being able to do so. Boiling takes time, fuel, and obviously a heatproof container. If you are able to boil your water, it should be filtered first to remove sediment and debris. This can be done using a coffee filter or even just a T-shirt.

FOOD

Bugging out is going to burn a lot of calories, and you can't always count on being able to hunt, fish, or trap your food while you're traveling. Instead, you'll have to bring at least some of those calories with you. I suggest avoiding the ever-popular MREs (Meals Ready to Eat) as they are heavy and bulky. Instead, concentrate on dehydrated/freeze-dried foods and also things that you can eat without any preparation.

Most dehydrated foods can be rehydrated with cold water. While this is not necessarily the tastiest thing you'll ever eat, it will fill bellies. Mountain House and Wise (www.FreezeDryGuy.com) are the more popular brands for these types of foods. They are light and contain a fair amount of nutrition, enabling you to fit several meals into a bug-out bag without much trouble.

Other food items for the bug-out bag include bagged tuna or chicken, crackers, dried fruits and nuts, granola bars, protein bars, and hard candy. Consider tossing in packets of instant coffee, tea bags, or drink mixes as well. Those won't take up much space at all and will certainly be welcome at the end of a long day of walking.

Don't forget utensils as well as ceramic or metal cups. How frustrating would it be to remember the instant coffee but be unable to drink it because all you have are liter bottles of water!

SHELTER

Next on the list is shelter. It is absolutely essential that you have a means of getting out of the elements. Hypothermia can set in quickly and with little warning. Regardless of how close your bug-out location may be, you should count on spending at least one or two nights under the stars until you get there. Carrying a full tent or two along with the rest of your gear might not be feasible, but that's OK because you don't necessarily need one; you can build simple shelters using a few space blankets and some paracord. Remember, the idea is just to be able to get by until you reach your bug-out location.

Incidentally, if you decide to pack space blankets in your bug-out bag, do yourself a favor and take them out of the package first. Unfold them, then refold them in a different way than they were originally packaged. If you don't, when you really need them, you may just find out that those fold lines have worn through and you'll be sitting there with nothing more than strips of material.

FIRE-MAKING

You may love the idea of starting a fire by rubbing two sticks together, but in reality, the easier it is for you to start your fire, the better off you will be. There are, of course, several primitive methods of fire-starting such as the bow drill, but a working butane lighter trumps them all. These are very cheap, so toss several into each bug-out bag. Remembering the Rule of Threes, don't stop there; add in magnesium strikers as well as old-fashioned flint and steel.

FIRE STRAWS

This is an ingenious way to transport tinder in a totally waterproof container. For this project, you'll need several plastic drinking straws (the wider the better), cotton balls, petroleum jelly, a candle, pliers, and toothpicks.

Place a good dollop of the petroleum jelly into a sandwich bag, then add a small handful of cotton balls. Squish it all together so the cotton balls become soaked with the jelly.

Cut the straws about in half or in thirds. Light the candle and hold one end of each cut straw a couple inches above the flame. When the plastic just begins to soften and melt, pull it away from the flame and crimp it closed with the pliers.

Then, using the toothpicks, begin working the cotton balls into the straws. Be patient and work slowly, adding just a bit of the cotton at a time. Once the straw is almost full, seal the open end just like you did before.

When you want to use them, simply cut a slit in the side of the straw and pull out some of the cotton strands. The cotton will light easily from either sparks or lighter flame. As it burns, the straw will melt, increasing the amount of flame being generated. These fire straws will burn long enough to get your smallest kindling started.

Packing some ready-to-use tinder is also a wise idea. The one time you truly need to start a fire, that old scoundrel Murphy will surely make an appearance and it will be pouring rain without a dry blade of grass to be found. Dryer lint is tried-and-true tinder, as are cotton balls soaked in petroleum jelly. Be sure to spend some time practicing getting a fire going under various weather conditions and using a variety of methods. Building a campfire is as much an art as it is a skill and few people can do it effectively the first time out.

Also included in the shelter category would be a few extra clothes, such as spare underwear and socks. If you've ever had to stomp through several inches of water on a hike, you know how incredibly welcome spare socks can be. A ball cap with a brim will help keep the sun off your face and sunglasses will cut the glare. Leather work gloves will protect your hands as you gather firewood for the night. All of these things take up very little space in the bug-out bag and add very little weight.

FIRST AID AND HYGIENE

Moving on to first aid, you can't expect to be able to carry a fully stocked trauma kit but there are several items that you should have with you on a bug out. You can start with a store-bought first aid kit but customize it by adding items for your individual situation. Adhesive bandages of all sizes should be standard, as should antibiotic ointment. Tweezers will help remove stubborn splinters. Elastic wrap will help with sprains. Cotton swabs, nitrile gloves, cold packs, and medical tape are also essentials. Don't forget pain relievers like ibuprofen, and you'll want to include extra prescription medicines if they are still available.

A good first aid manual will be beneficial if no one in your group is a fully trained paramedic, nurse, or doctor. One of the best books currently available is *The Doom and Bloom™ Survival Medicine Handbook* by Joseph Alton, M.D.

and Amy Alton, A.R.N.P. A close second would be a copy of the *Special Forces Medical Handbook*.

Other nice things to have are lip balm and sunscreen, both of which will help mitigate the effects of being out in the elements for possibly days on end. Insect repellent may also be desirable. In my area, the skeeters come large enough to qualify as small-engine aircraft.

As for hygiene, you can't expect to be able to take a full bath or shower, of course, when you're on the run. But having the means to wash up is not only sanitary, it is a tremendous morale boost. In each bug-out bag, include hand sanitizer to be used after urinating or defecating. A small washcloth can be used to take a quick sponge bath, with a dishtowel used to dry off if need be. A hotel-sized bar of soap will take up very little space and be much appreciated. Another essential is a roll or two of toilet paper. You can reduce the bulk by removing the cardboard tube and smashing the roll flat, then placing it in a plastic zip-top bag to keep it dry.

SECURITY

Each adult bug-out bag should contain a firearm and ammunition. Naturally, given that a bug-out bag is typically a backpack, these will probably be handguns. Should you have the opportunity to do so as you evacuate, you'd want to grab rifles and shotguns as well as ammunition for them. But, in the event that is not possible, having firearms stashed in the bug-out bags will prevent you from being helpless. Don't forget holsters and cleaning kits for each firearm.

OTHER ITEMS

There are a few additional items that don't fit into one of those categories but will be extremely helpful:

A good quality sheath knife is critical. Personally, I like to have two blades. The first, a kukri knife, is used for cutting through brush, batoning large branches for firewood, and other camp chores. The other is a small sheath knife with a 5-inch blade. This is what I'd use for skinning game, cleaning fish, and other tasks that don't require a heavy blade.

Duct tape has innumerable uses, from clothing and shelter repair to attaching items to your pack. You can wrap the duct tape around a pencil or other thin dowel to cut down the weight and size of the roll.

A small pry bar may come in handy should you need to force your way through a gate or door.

BATONING WOOD

This is a technique used when all the available firewood is wet. It takes a long time for moisture to seep through to the middle of dead wood. Therefore, even though the large branches you find on the ground are very wet on the outside, there is dry wood in there that you can use, even if it has been sitting in a puddle for a few days.

This method works best on branches that are about 5 feet in length or smaller. Stand the branch up on its end and place a thick-bladed knife at the top. Using another branch, pound the knife down through the wood, splitting it lengthwise. You can do this several times with the branch, producing a quantity of splintered dry wood.

A good multi-tool, such as a Leatherman, is always useful.

Fish hooks, sinkers, and several dozen feet of fishing line wrapped around a sewing bobbin will fit into an old 35mm film canister and could be invaluable in procuring food.

You may also consider adding to each bug-out bag a small quantity of silver or gold coins. While I am not as gung-ho as some other survivalists on the subject of stockpiling precious metals, I cannot deny the potential value they may have to a family bugging out. The ideal on a bug out would be to be able to avoid contact with anyone until you reach your destination. But, should you come across an individual or group, you may be able to barter some coins for food or shelter if needed.

Once you reach your bug-out location, concentrate your efforts on starting anew. Be thankful for the second chance.

CHAPTER 15

Excursions

While perhaps not in the first few days after a collapse, at some point you or members of your team will find it necessary to leave the retreat for one reason or another. Excursions need to be planned in advance, as much as possible, in order to mitigate the inherent risks. In this chapter we'll explore what types of things you need to think about.

Reasons for Excursions

There are several reasons why you might send team members out into the world. Gathering intelligence is probably the number-one most common one. As we've discussed elsewhere, the retreat is not a universe unto itself. There is a big, wide world out there and prudent preppers will want to learn as much as they can about it. Doing so will most likely entail sending members of the team out to explore and see what's what. For our purposes here, we'll refer to those team members as scouts.

Patrolling falls under the category of intelligence gathering. You may not necessarily have team members walking the perimeter and beyond on a constant basis;

few retreats will be able to provide the necessary manpower to pull that off. However, it is a wise idea to have team members routinely go out beyond the perimeter and scout the surrounding area for potential threats. We'll go into more detail on patrolling later.

Another major reason for excursions will be to scrounge up needed supplies. This brings up the looting versus scavenging debate, which is one that lands squarely in what we might call a gray area. Some people look at it as outright theft, no matter what is taken, from where it is taken, or why. At the other end of the spectrum are those who say that in a world without law, anything goes. Suffice it to say, many retreat groups may find it necessary to send out scouts to locate certain items at one point or another.

Better to prepare for that possibility than discount it out of hand.

A third reason for an excursion will be to make contact with other survivors. Once you've determined that a surviving group exists in your area and doesn't appear to be a direct threat to your own group, you may be able to set up a mutual aid agreement with them, as we discussed in Chapter 12. There is also barter to consider. If none of your chickens made it through the disaster but the other group has several, both groups may be amenable to trading eggs for bread, for example. Naturally, making contact with another group is a risky proposition. However, in most cases I think groups will be interested in networking with one another, for safety if nothing else.

Excursion Planning and Protocol

Any excursion should be planned out extensively. The scouts should be those team members who are swiftest on their feet and best able to blend in with the surrounding

LOOTING VERSUS SCAVENGING

A very common scene in end-of-the-world fiction is when the hero of the piece, down to his last bullet and bit of food, comes across an abandoned convenience store or some other former retail establishment. There, despite it having obviously been ransacked countless times, he finds just what he needs: a few cans of food, a bottle or two of water, and oh-so-convenient, a shotgun, complete with a box of shells. If he's really lucky, perhaps a new trench coat to replace the one lost in the last gun battle. Having recharged his batteries, so to speak, he heads back out into the wastelands to go toe-to-toe with the head of the MZB gang.

Here in the real world, most of us saw photos and video shot in New Orleans after Hurricane Katrina swept through the area. There were countless images of people stealing TVs and other electronic items from smashed store windows.

Why would we look at one of those scenarios any different from the other?

In my opinion, there is a vast, yet simple, difference between looting and scavenging. Let's put it this way.

Taking food for your child = scavenging.

Taking a 60" HDTV = looting.

If the items taken have no clear ownership—if they are found in an abandoned wreck of a store, for example—and populace. They should be intelligent and able to think on their feet, make swift decisions, and act on them.

It is of the utmost importance that your scouts have intimate knowledge of the area. Any available maps should be memorized as much as possible. As they prog-

they will serve to keep you and your family alive, I'd consider it scavenging. On the other hand, if the items are clearly owned by someone else and/or serve no purpose other than just being inherently valuable, that's looting.

Obviously, the whole point of prepping is to set aside what you'll need, come what may. However, there are any number of reasons why scavenging may become important. Perhaps much of your food storage was destroyed in a flood or became infested with pests. Or maybe an illness has swept through the retreat, depleting your stored medicines.

There are many people who insist they would never take a single thing that didn't belong to them, often citing the Eighth Commandment. My counter-argument to that is, if you are devout enough to truly strive to follow the Ten Commandments, then surely you are enough of a believer to recognize the possibility that God may have put you on the path to the abandoned store that sits in front of you. Perhaps this is His way of ensuring that you and your family live for another day.

Bear in mind, I'm not advocating that anyone go out pillaging the countryside the minute law and order break down. What I am saying is that scavenging and scrounging for supplies may become a matter of course in a world without rule of law.

ress through exploring the neighborhood and beyond, the maps should be updated to reflect known trouble spots, occupied homes and buildings, and other details that may become important later. This knowledge will help your team members avoid detection by being able to work their way around potential enemies.

Scouts should also be kept appraised of the needs of the group. Provide them with "shopping lists" before they head out. Be sure they have the means to transport those items if they are found, for instance carrying an empty knapsack in their bag when they head out.

Plan out with your scouts where they will go and how they will get there. While these routes are not to be considered set in stone, the scouts should stick with the plan as much as possible. This way if they don't return when expected, the remaining team members will know where to begin searching.

SCOUT SURVIVAL KITS

Every scout should carry with them a survival kit, just in case they are unable to make it back to the retreat in a short amount of time. These kits should contain, at a minimum:

FOOD   If you were packing such a kit today, you'd include things like granola bars and dried nuts. Post-collapse, it might be some dried meat and dandelion leaves. The important thing is to have sustenance in the kit in case the scout gets stranded or delayed due to weather or other reasons. Food procurement supplies are a good idea as well, but the focus for the scouts will be to get to their destination and back to the retreat as quickly as possible.

WATER At least one liter of potable water, along with the means to filter and purify more.

FIRST AID SUPPLIES A small but well-stocked first aid kit is essential. Climbing in and around rubble and debris will undoubtedly lead to injuries such as cuts and scrapes. The quicker these injuries are addressed, the lower the chance of infection.

TOOLS Scouts should have with them a variety of tools that will be helpful in their tasks. These include such things as small pry bars, flashlights, screwdrivers, and pliers. Avoid weighing them down with too much heavy-duty equipment, though. Scouts may need to move swiftly and quietly, which is difficult to do when carrying an entire toolbox.

MAPS AND NOTEPADS Make sure scouts have the means to take notes as needed, rather than having to rely strictly upon memory. Having maps of the area will allow them to compare what is in a location now rather than what was there pre-collapse. Do not, however, have the location of your retreat noted on the map in any way, shape, or form. Should the map get lost or taken, you do not want to compromise your position.

FIRE-STARTING KIT Should the scout be forced to spend a night away from the retreat, the individual situation will dictate whether it is safe and prudent to have a campfire. But it's better to have a fire-starting kit and not need it than need it and not have it. This kit should include at least three ways to spark a fire, such as a butane lighter, strike-anywhere matches, and a magnesium block with a flint rod attached. It should also have ready-to-use tinder like cotton balls smeared with petroleum jelly or fire straws, as discussed in Chapter 14.

EMERGENCY SHELTER SUPPLIES   While ducking into an abandoned building may suffice, there may be compelling reasons for not doing so. Therefore, scouts should carry space blankets or some other means of cobbling together a quick shelter for an overnight stay.

COMMUNICATIONS   Scouts should be provided with two-way radios so they are able to communicate with each other as well as with the rest of the team at the retreat. This may be crucial if, for example, a scout sees indications that the retreat is about to receive a visit from an armed contingent of the local Welcome Wagon.

WEAPONS   Scouts should, of course, be armed. However, as we'll discuss shortly in the section on avoiding detection, it may not be prudent to be visibly armed to the teeth. A concealed handgun and ample ammunition may suffice.

If possible, your scouts should wear thick-soled boots to prevent puncture wounds from broken glass and other debris. They should also carry leather work gloves to avoid injuries to the hands as they climb through any rubble or dilapidated buildings. As noted earlier, be sure to include an empty knapsack or some other means of transporting items the scouts find back to the retreat.

EXITING THE PERIMETER

Prior to scouts leaving the secured perimeter, the team members acting as lookouts should observe the immediate area and make sure an exit is safe. Scouts should exit quickly but quietly, with the ideal being a gradual fading away rather than a quick sprint. The lookouts should continue their observations and pay particular attention to the movements of the scouts for as long as they are visible. The lookouts should, of course, alert the scouts to anything amiss.

Preferably, the exit from the perimeter should not take place where the scouts will easily be seen and noticed. In a rural area, this may not be a big concern, since if anyone were close enough to see the scouts leave, they'd probably be close enough to already know about the retreat itself. In an urban area, though, scouts should not walk out the front gate but instead slip through a back exit.

AVOIDING DETECTION

At all times where it is feasible to do so, the scouts should strive to remain unnoticed. Most of the time, this will involve keeping movement low-key and constantly scanning the area for potential threats of discovery. However, there may also be occasions where blending in and being unobtrusive will be the ideal.

In today's society, if one were to visit the local mall while wearing combat fatigues, carrying a large pack, and armed to the teeth, it would certainly bring about lots of attention. However, if the same person were to walk into the mall wearing jeans with an untucked button-down shirt and carrying a messenger bag, few would look twice. No one would probably realize the untucked shirt conceals a handgun at the small of the back and the bag contains bug-out gear. Post-collapse, this may mean wearing ratty clothes with holes, rather than the comparatively clean and neat attire to which your preps have allowed you access.

Regardless of how vacant an area may appear to be, scouts should take measures to avoid loud noise and other telltale signs of their presence. Should it be necessary to force their way into a building, they should do so as quickly and quietly as possible. Rather than kicking in a door, for example, look for a ground level window that could be forced open. The sound of a single pane of glass being broken will not carry nearly as far as that of a door being kicked, especially if the kick is repeated out of necessity until the door opens.

If this is a scavenging mission, the scouts should get in, get what they need, and get out. While they should make note of items they may wish to come back for at a later time, they should concentrate on the task at hand. Every minute they spend outside the retreat is an increase in risk not only to themselves but to their family and team back home. Should their presence be discovered, they may be followed back to the retreat, exposing everyone to danger. They could also be captured, likely leading to serious injury, possibly death. The watchwords are get in, get out, and leave as little trace as possible.

RETURNING TO THE RETREAT

Unless circumstances dictate otherwise, scouts should not travel in a direct line back to the retreat. Instead, they should take a more roundabout route to make sure they are not being followed. If they believe they are being tailed in some way, they should travel in a direction away from the retreat while trying to throw off the tail.

In an urban area, this may mean ducking in and out of buildings and doubling back here and there. In a more rural area, the scouts should attempt to outdistance their new friends, then circle back in a wide arc. When possible, they should communicate with the team members back at the retreat to keep them up to date on the situation.

Upon safely arriving near the perimeter, the lookouts should pay close attention to determine whether the scouts have been followed. If need be, the long-range rifles may be used to dissuade further pursuit. While this course of action will more or less give away the fact that the retreat is occupied and possibly well-armed, at this point it's probably no longer a secret anyway.

PATROLS

While patrols could be considered part of your perimeter defensive measures, given that they entail team members leaving the retreat "safe zone," I'm including them here. Few groups will have the resources to allow team members to routinely be out patrolling the area around the perimeter. Your group has a finite number of people and each of them will likely already be performing several functions, from tending gardens and livestock to building maintenance to just plain surviving. But when feasible, it is a great idea to routinely send out patrols to observe the area around the retreat. They provide another set of eyes to complement your lookouts.

Should you have the ability to send out patrols, they should not walk the same route every time, nor should they do anything else that would cause them to be predictable. Have them vary their routines every time they are out and about.

On the other hand, if the scouts do indeed appear to be alone, there should be some way for them to communicate their well-being to the team inside the retreat prior to being allowed access back inside. This is to prevent a scout from being forced to provide access to the perimeter by enemies.

A simple way to communicate that all is well may be to give each scout a purple bandana. As they approach the retreat, this bandana is to be stuck in a back pocket with the end trailing out. If the retreat team sees the bandana, they know all is well. No bandana means something is up and they should proceed with caution. A bandana is innocuous enough that if it were found in the backpack of a captured scout, it wouldn't be seen as out of the ordinary. Code words and phrases, as discussed in Chapter 11, are another way of accomplishing the same goal.

By the same token, the scouts should receive some sort of confirming signal from inside the perimeter to verify that everything is copacetic with the rest of the team. Again, this could be a visual signal like a specific hand gesture or the display of a colored bandana. A code word or phrase may fit the bill as well.

AVOID SOLO EXCURSIONS

It is never a good idea to allow scouts to work solo. Remember, this is real life, not Hollywood. As such, sending out someone on their own without backup is not going to end well in many cases. Keeping the scouts in groups of two or three will allow them to watch each other's backs while still remaining reasonably stealthy.

Excursions

Be sure to have contingency plans in place in case the scouts get separated for some reason. Establish various rallying points where they can meet within a specified time frame before heading back to the retreat. Have one or two rallying points in each area where the scouts will be headed. For example, if you are in a relatively urban area, divide the surrounding area on your map into four or five sections. Each section should have at least one rallying point. If the scouts are separated, they should work toward the rallying point in that section. Should a scout not arrive within a given time frame, say two hours, those who did make it should proceed to the retreat.

APPENDICES

Further Reading

It would be almost impossible to include every last scrap of good information related to disaster readiness in a single source. I encourage all preppers and survivalists to put together a comprehensive library of material they can utilize as needed. In this section, I've listed a number of books as well as blogs and websites. Each has been selected for specific reasons and all are highly recommended.

Books

Each of the books listed here is currently available as of this writing. None is out of print or otherwise difficult to obtain. While there is some overlap in information presented in these books, all are excellent references to have on hand, both now and after a crisis.

Bug Out: The Complete Plan for Escaping a Catastrophic Disaster Before It's Too Late by Scott B. Williams
Williams is the rare survival author who has truly been there and done that. *Bug Out* isn't a traditional survival manual in that the focus isn't so much on how to survive, but where to go to better

your chances of survival. Williams breaks up the continental United States into several regions. For each, he gives critical information on climate, flora, fauna, and other factors that are of concern to the survivalist. He also suggests several specific areas in each region that might be ideal for bugging out.

Build the Perfect Bug Out Bag: Your 72-Hour Disaster Survival Kit by Creek Stewart
This is my number one recommended book for making survival kits at home. Stewart covers every possible need one would have in a disaster and shows the reader how to meet those needs with items easily transported in a kit. He not only gives you lists of items to include but explains why you need them in the kit and how to use them effectively.

Emergency Food Storage & Survival Handbook: Everything You Need to Know to Keep Your Family Safe in a Crisis by Peggy Lawton
If you are a checklist person, this is *the* book to have for preparing for emergencies large and small. Lawton gives the reader a ton of practical information, concentrating on family preparedness. While much of the book centers on food storage, there is also information on all the little things that should be stored ahead of time to make life easier down the road.

Further Reading

The Doom and Bloom™ Survival Medicine Handbook by
Joseph Alton, M.D. and Amy Alton, A.R.N.P.
This is probably the most comprehensive book
I've seen that specifically addresses medical needs
during and after a catastrophe. Dr. Alton and
Amy Alton are known to their fans as Dr. Bones
and Nurse Amy. What I particularly like is their
inclusion of herbal remedies, information that could
be vital when pharmacies are no longer available.

The Encyclopedia of Country Living by Carla Emery
Sustainable living and self-reliance go hand in hand
with preparedness. After all, if you are growing and
raising your own food, you're ahead of the game
should the unthinkable happen. This book is often
considered the bible for homesteaders. Just about
every topic imaginable is covered, from growing
crops to butchering fowl.

*The Prepper's Pocket Guide: 101 Easy Things You Can Do to
Ready Your Home for a Disaster* by Bernie Carr
This is a great little book for those just starting
out with prepping. Each of the 101 things listed
in the book are easily managed by most folks.
The emphasis is on those things one can do for
themselves, often for little money.

The Unthinkable: Who Survives When Disaster Strikes—and Why by Amanda Ripley

As far as I'm concerned, this book should be required reading for anyone who fancies themselves a prepper or survivalist. In this book, Ripley uses real-life examples of major disasters, such as the sinking of the *Titanic*, and explains how the human responses to stress in a crisis can both help and hinder survival. She participated in research studies herself and interviewed several experts to determine how some of those biological impulses can be harnessed and used to better effect.

Blogs and Websites

While these sites and discussion groups may not be entirely focused on issues relating to security and defense, those topics do come up frequently. All of them are centered upon disaster readiness, emergency preparedness, and potential world-without-rule-of-law scenarios. Obviously, with the Internet being ever-changing, there is no way to guarantee these links will still work years from now. But as of the time of this writing, each site listed is up and running.

Survival Weekly

www.SurvivalWeekly.com

This is my primary website. The focus is on both short- and long-term prepping. I also maintain a blog titled The Library at the End of the World where I review books and movies of interest to survivalists.

Survival-Gear Blog

www.Survival-Gear.com/blog

My daily blog, updated every weekday. Blog posts run the gamut from first aid kit recommendations to the differences between being a prepper and being a survivalist.

American Preppers Network

www.AmericanPreppersNetwork.com

This site strives to be something akin to the CNN of prepping and they are well on their way to achieving that goal. It is updated frequently with new articles on a very wide range of topics.

Survival Blog

www.SurvivalBlog.com

Probably the most popular survival-related site on the Web. Started and still maintained by James Wesley, Rawles, it offers a ton of excellent information for both the budding and the experienced survivalist.

Bug Out Survival

www.BugOutSurvival.com

An excellent blog written by noted survival author Scott B. Williams. As I frequently say when I review his books, he has truly been there and done that when it comes to wilderness survival techniques.

Recommended Suppliers

At last count, there are approximately umpteen bazillion companies out there selling survival-related gear. If you pay close attention, though, you'll see that many of those stores are all selling the same stuff from the same sources. In fact, there are many stores that really stock no products at all; they are merely intermediaries between the customer and the supplier. Personally, I prefer to deal with companies who know their product lines inside and out, know what works and what doesn't, and have staff with the practical experience and knowledge to make recommendations suited to the customer's specific needs.

What follows is a short list of companies that I've either done business with personally or have been recommended to me by trusted friends and colleagues. The failure to include any specific company here is not meant to be in any way a slight against them. It just means that I don't know enough about them to personally recommend them.

Cheaper Than Dirt

www.CheaperThanDirt.com

They bill themselves as "America's Ultimate Shooting Sports Discounter" and I'm inclined to agree. Their prices on ammo and firearms accessories can rarely be beat.

Cold Steel

www.ColdSteel.com

I'm a big fan of Cold Steel products. They first became popular back in the 1980s with a line of tanto knives and haven't looked back since. Extremely tough and durable, each blade design is rigorously tested before being made available for purchase. I've owned a few of their products over the years and have never once been disappointed.

Emergency Essentials

BePrepared.com

Often seen as the "go to" source for a wide range of disaster-readiness supplies, Emergency Essentials has great prices on the items they have in stock.

ESEE Knives

www.EseeKnives.com

Another excellent blade manufacturer. Every knife they sell is made with top-of-the-line materials and extreme attention to detail. They know what works and have eliminated what doesn't.

FreezeDryGuy

www.FreezeDryGuy.com

FreezeDryGuy was one of the first companies in the United States to sell freeze-dried foods to the general public. Since then, they have developed into a very well-known supplier of food packaged for extreme long-term conditions. Of all the companies with whom I've ever dealt, their customer service easily ranks in the Top 5. They also seem to always have products in stock, even when other similar suppliers are having trouble filling orders.

I.C.E. Cord

www.ICEcord.com

I.C.E. stands for In Case of Emergency. If it can be made with paracord, I.C.E. Cord makes and sells it. If you don't see what you need on their site, they'll do custom work as well. Their product line includes bracelets, monkey fists, lanyards, slings, even watchbands. Given the incredibly diverse uses for paracord in a survival situation, having an extra dozen feet stashed on your wrist is never a bad idea.

JG Sales

www.JGsales.com

This site offers great prices on both new and used firearms, though remember you'll need to factor in the cost of transfer fees for your local FFL (Federal Firearms License) dealer. Their website is very well organized and it is easy to find exactly what you are seeking.

LPC Survival

www.Directive21.com

Jeff and his team at LPC Survival know more about water purification than anyone else around. An authorized distributor of Berkey water filtration products, they provide their customers with solid recommendations on what will work the best in their unique circumstances.

Survival-Gear

www.Survival-Gear.com

Survival-Gear offers a wide range of preparedness supplies, from snare wire all the way to complete survival kits. Fair prices and the customer service can't be beat.

TBO-Tech

www.TBOtech.com

TBO-Tech specializes in security and defense products for the home and business, including everything from wireless surveillance cameras to stun guns.

Photo Credits

About the Author

JIM COBB has worked in the investigation and security fields for twenty years and has been a survivalist most of his life. His articles on preparedness have been published in national magazines such as *Boy's Life*. You can find him online at www.SurvivalWeekly.com as well as blogging for www.Survival-Gear.com. Jim lives in the upper Midwest with his beautiful wife and their three adolescent weapons of mass destruction.

More Great Books from Jim Cobb

Prepper's Long-Term
Survival Guide

Countdown to
Preparedness

Prepper's Financial Guide

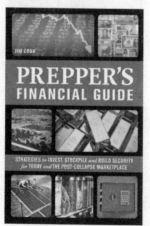

Prepper's Survival Hacks

Get more info at:
www.ulyssespress.com/survival